The Sign of the Four

Sir Arthur Conan Doyle

Level 3
(1600-word)

JN086661

IBC パブリッシング

はじめに

　ラダーシリーズは、「はしご（ladder）」を使って一歩一歩上を目指すように、学習者の実力に合わせ、無理なくステップアップできるよう開発された英文リーダーのシリーズです。

　リーディング力をつけるためには、繰り返したくさん読むこと、いわゆる「多読」がもっとも効果的な学習法であると言われています。多読では、「1. 速く　2. 訳さず英語のまま　3. なるべく辞書を使わず」に読むことが大切です。スピードを計るなど、速く読むよう心がけましょう（たとえば TOEIC® テストの音声スピードはおよそ 1 分間に 150語です）。そして 1 語ずつ訳すのではなく、英語を英語のまま理解するくせをつけるようにします。こうして読み続けるうちに語感がついてきて、だんだんと英語が理解できるようになるのです。まずは、ラダーシリーズの中からあなたのレベルに合った本を選び、少しずつ英文に慣れ親しんでください。たくさんの本を手にとるうちに、英文書がすらすら読めるようになってくるはずです。

《本シリーズの特徴》

- 中学校レベルから中級者レベルまで5段階に分かれています。自分に合ったレベルからスタートしてください。
- クラシックから現代文学、ノンフィクション、ビジネスと幅広いジャンルを扱っています。あなたの興味に合わせてタイトルを選べます。
- 巻末のワードリストで、いつでもどこでも単語の意味を確認できます。レベル1、2では、文中の全ての単語が、レベル3以上は中学校レベル外の単語が掲載されています。
- カバーにヘッドホーンマークのついているタイトルは、オーディオ・サポートがあります。ウェブから購入／ダウンロードし、リスニング教材としても併用できます。

《使用語彙について》

レベル1：中学校で学習する単語約1000語

レベル2：レベル1の単語＋使用頻度の高い単語約300語

レベル3：レベル1の単語＋使用頻度の高い単語約600語

レベル4：レベル1の単語＋使用頻度の高い単語約1000語

レベル5：語彙制限なし

CONTENTS

読みはじめる前に

[物語の解説]

    The Sign of the Four（四つの署名）は、シャーロック・ホームズシリーズの長編小説の一つで、ホームズとワトソンの初めての出会いを描いた『緋色の研究』に続くシリーズ第二作です。

    作品は当初、*The Sign of the Four; or, the Problem of the Sholtos*（四つの署名、もしくはショルトー一族の問題）という題名で発表されました。日本では、『四つの署名』、『四つのサイン』、『四人の署名』等のタイトルが使われています。Chapter 1 から Chapter 11 までで事件を、最後の Chapter 12 で犯行に至った動機を描いています。

    この小説の最後でワトソンは依頼者のメアリー・モースタンと結婚し、ホームズとの共同生活を一度終わらせたことになっています。

[物語のあらすじ]

    この数ヵ月ろくな事件が起きず暇を持てあましていたホームズのもとに、若い女性が訪ねてくる。

    女性の名前はメアリー・モースタン。彼女の父親はインドで従軍していたが、10 年ほど前に休暇でロンドンに帰国した後、行方不明となってしまった。そして 6 年前から、

毎年同じ日に正体不明の人物から彼女のもとへ大粒の真珠が送られてくるようになった。さらに「未知の友」を名乗る謎の人物から面会を求める手紙が届いたことから、ホームズに相談をしにきたのだ。

　彼女に同行したホームズとワトソンは、手紙の差出人から彼女の父親の過去にまつわる話を聞き、そして真珠の持ち主が判明する。しかし持ち主を訪ねてみると、すでに殺されており、そこには「四つの署名」が残されていた。

　ホームズは犯人の正体を突き止め、犯人とホームズとの追走劇がテムズ河で繰り広げられる。そして明らかになる「四つの署名」の真相と、過去から現在へとつながる事件の全貌とは――。

[単語リスト]

本書で使われている用語です。わからない語は巻末のワードリストで確認しましょう。

- ☐ agate
- ☐ blowpipe
- ☐ cover-up
- ☐ creosote
- ☐ foothold
- ☐ governor-general
- ☐ halting
- ☐ rajah
- ☐ reasoning
- ☐ rediscovery
- ☐ rudder
- ☐ sahib
- ☐ short-handed
- ☐ sideburn
- ☐ Sikh
- ☐ sill
- ☐ theorist
- ☐ underlie

[主な登場人物]

Sherlock Holmes シャーロック・ホームズ　鋭い観察眼と推理力、そして犯罪に関する膨大な知識をあわせ持つ私立探偵。ロンドンのベーカー街221Bに下宿している。

John H. Watson ジョン・H・ワトソン　医師。ホームズの相棒でこの物語の語り手。ベーカー街221Bでホームズと同居している。

Mary Morstan メアリー・モースタン　本件の依頼人。父のモースタン大尉が失踪した後、毎年同じ日に真珠が差出人不明で届くようになる。

Captain Morstan モースタン大尉　メアリーの父。アンダマン諸島囚人警備隊の将校。休暇のためにロンドンに帰国後、謎の失踪を遂げる。

Major John Sholto ジョン・ショルトー少佐　モースタン大尉の友人。かつて同じ連隊に所属していた退役軍人。

Thaddeus Sholto サディアス・ショルトー　ショルトー少佐の息子。メアリーに面会を求める手紙を送り、同行したホームズたちにモースタン大尉とショルトー少佐の因縁話を聞かせる。

Bartholomew Sholto バーソロミュー・ショルトー　サディアスの双子の兄。ポンディシェリー荘で毒矢を受けて死亡しているのが見つかる。

Jonathan Small ジョナサン・スモール　義足の男。モースタン大尉の遺品とポンディシェリー荘の現場に残されていた「四つの署名」の筆頭にあった名前。

Athelney Jones アセルニー・ジョーンズ　ロンドン警視庁の刑事。

The Sign of the Four

Chapter 1
The Science of Deduction

Sherlock Holmes took his cocaine bottle from the shelf and his needle from the case. He pulled up his sleeve and put the needle in his arm. I had wanted to stop him from doing this many times but could not say anything. He knew taking this drug was bad for his body, but it excited his mind. He liked his mind to be very active

and said that was why he chose to be the world's only unofficial consulting detective.

He thought that deduction should be an exact science. He believed he was the only person to have the three qualities necessary for the ideal detective — the power to look, the power to think, and the power of knowledge. He told me, for example, how important it is to be able to know the difference among the ashes of the various tobaccos and the tracing of footsteps.

I did not quite understand the difference between looking and thinking. He explained by telling me that this morning I went to the post office and sent a telegram.

"How did you know?" I asked.

"By looking, I see you have some red dirt on your shoe," he started. "Workmen are repairing the street near the post office where such red dirt is found. I also know that you have not written a letter or used any of my postcards or stamps. The only reason for going to the post office, then, was to send a telegram — this was the thinking part."

I then tested him by showing him my watch and asking him to tell me about the man who had owned it before me. I was sure I could prove that he was not as clever as he thought. But by examining the details of the watch he was, indeed, able to tell me that it had belonged to my elder brother and, moreover, what kind of man he was. I couldn't believe my ears! Before I could ask him more about it, there was a knock on the door — someone to see Holmes, a Miss Mary Morstan.

Chapter 2
The Statement of the Case

Miss Morstan came in. She was a young, blonde lady and was well dressed. She seemed very upset. She said she was in a very strange situation, almost impossible to explain.

"My father was in the army in India and he sent me home to England when I was still a small child," she began. "My mother was dead and she had no family here, so I was placed in a boarding house owned by a Mrs. Forrester. In 1878 my father returned to England for a year. I received a telegram from him telling me to meet him at his hotel in London. It had been many years since I had

seen him and I was very
excited. But when I got
there he was not there.
He had checked into the
hotel, but he went out
the day before I arrived
and never came back.
The date was December
3, 1878."

Holmes was listening
carefully and nodded his head for her to
continue. "Even stranger," she said, "was
about six years ago—to be exact, on May
4, 1882—an ad appeared in the newspaper
asking for the address of Miss Mary Morstan,
stating that it would be to her advantage to
come forward."

She told us that she published her address
in the ad column and on the same day a
box arrived in the mail. It contained a very
large and beautiful pearl, but no note or any
letter. Since then every year on the same date
a box has always arrived, always containing

a similar pearl, without any clue as to the sender. The pearls were said to be of a rare variety and of great value. She showed us the six pearls and the wrapping they arrived in. She was sure the writing on the wrapping was not her father's.

"This is very interesting," said Holmes. "Has anything else happened to you?"

"Yes, just today. That is why I have come to you. This morning I received this letter, which you will perhaps read for yourself." Holmes examined the envelope carefully. The letter read:

> Be at the third pillar from the left outside the Lyceum Theatre tonight at 7:00. If you are distrustful, bring two friends. You are a wronged woman and shall have justice. Do not bring police. If you do, it will all be for nothing.
>
> Your unknown friend.

She needed help, so Holmes and I decided

to go with her to the theater. She said she would be back at 6:00 and left.

"What a very pretty woman!" I said, turning to Holmes.

"Is she?" he replied. "I did not look."

Holmes had to go out for a while. I sat in his chair thinking about the young lady. I was charmed by her beauty and thought she must now be 27 if she had been 17 at the time of her father's disappearance. But what was I but a poor doctor with an even poorer leg? Not a great match for a woman like her.

Chapter 3
Looking for a Solution

Holmes came back at 5:30 and he was in a good mood. He thought that he already had an important clue to the mystery. Mary's father had only one friend in London, a Major Sholto. They had been together in India. Holmes checked the back files of the Times and learned that Sholto had died on April 28, 1882.

Within a week of this date, Mary got the package with the pearl and this was repeated every year. He wondered if one of Sholto's relatives was sending the presents and had now sent the letter.

Mary arrived and the three of us went out for our strange meeting. Holmes asked her more about Sholto. She said he and her father had spent time in the Andaman Islands, just off the coast of India. She also said that a strange piece of paper had been found in her father's desk which no one could understand. She showed it to Holmes, who examined it carefully. It seemed to be a map of a large building. At one point there was a red cross and above it was written '3.37 from left' in pencil. In the left-hand corner was a strange symbol, like four crosses in a line with their arms touching. Beside it was written 'The sign of the four—Jonathan Small, Mahomet Singh, Abdullah Khan, Dost Akbar.' Holmes did not know what it meant but thought it was important.

There were many people at the Lyceum Theatre

and just as we reached the third pillar, the place of the meeting, a small, dark man came up to us.

"Are you the people who came with Miss Morstan?" he asked.

"I am Miss Morstan and these two gentlemen are my friends," she said.

He asked if we were policemen and she replied we were not.

"Then you must come with me to meet my employer."

A horse-drawn cab pulled up and we got in and raced away through the foggy streets. We drove and drove and did not know where we were going, except Holmes, who knew every area that we went through.

We came to a poor neighborhood and stopped at a house which was dark inside except for a little light in the kitchen window. All of the neighboring houses were dark and looked empty. On knocking, a Hindu servant opened the door.

"The sahib awaits you," he said.

We heard a high-pitched voice from an inner room which said, "Show them in, quickly."

Chapter 4
The Story of
the Bald-Headed Man

We followed the Indian down a dark hall until he opened a door on the right. Inside the room was a small man with almost no hair at all. His teeth were yellow and, as he spoke, he tried to cover his mouth with his hand. The furniture, paintings, and decorations inside his room did not match the rest of the house. They were clearly those of a rich man.

The bald man introduced himself as Mr. Thaddeus Sholto. "I will tell you everything that happened. My father was Major John Sholto, once of the Indian Army. He retired

11 years ago and came back to England to live with my twin brother Bartholomew and me. We read about the disappearance of Captain Morstan, but we did not know our father was keeping a secret about what had really happened to him." Holmes and Mary and I were paying close attention to his every word.

"Early in 1882," Thaddeus said, "my father received a letter from India which was a great shock to him. My brother and I did not know what the letter said, but it made our father very sick. His condition got worse, and towards the end of April he wished to say some last words to us. He confessed that he had a treasure, that he had kept it all for himself but should have given at least half to Morstan's daughter, Mary. He felt very bad about what he had done. He asked us to send Mary a fair share of the treasure, but only after he had died."

"My father and Captain Morstan had discovered this treasure in India. My father brought it to England, and when Captain

Morstan returned to London he came to our house to get his share. He and my father argued about how much each should get. Morstan yelled in anger, fell backward and cut his head on the corner of the treasure chest. He died right there in the room."

I looked over at Mary and saw tears in her eyes. But she nodded for Thaddeus to continue.

"Of course, my father knew people would think he killed his friend. His servant and he decided to hide the body, and within a few days the London newspapers were full of the mysterious disappearance of Captain Morstan. Now, as he was dying, he wanted to do the right thing by giving Mary her part. He asked my brother and me to put our ears down to his mouth and said, 'The treasure is hidden in —'

"At this moment his face became filled with fear and he said in a very loud voice, 'Keep him out!' We turned our heads in the direction he was looking, and through the window we could see a wild, angry face looking in. We ran over to the window, but the man was gone. When we returned to the bed, our father was dead."

Thaddeus then told us more about the mystery. "We found one footmark outside the window, so we knew we had not imagined the face. In the morning the same window was open and we saw that someone had opened all the boxes and cupboards in the room. On top of our father's chest was a torn piece of paper with the words 'The sign of the four' written on it. We did not know who had come inside or what the words meant. It did not look like anything had been stolen."

After listening to all of this Mary turned white, but when I offered her some water, she recovered somewhat.

Thaddeus told us how excited he and his brother were about the treasure. For years they had looked for it in the garden but could not find it. The only part of the treasure they had seen were the pearls their father kept in his room. Bartholomew was like his father and did not want to part with the pearls. They both thought that, by sending them to Mary, they might get in trouble.

Finally, they decided to send one pearl a year. Still, they could not agree completely, so Thaddeus decided to live separately from his brother. Then, yesterday, he learned that the treasure had been found, and he wrote the letter to Mary to meet him.

Now Thaddeus asked us to drive to his father's house with him and demand a share of the treasure from Bartholomew. Thaddeus thought it was valued at £500,000. Our eyes went big upon hearing this amount. Even with just half of this, Miss Morstan would become the richest lady in England.

Chapter 5

The Tragedy of Pondicherry Lodge

It was nearly 11:00 when we reached the final stage of our night's adventures. We had come to Pondicherry Lodge in Norwood, where Bartholomew lived. The doorman didn't want to let us in, but, after much conversation we were allowed to go inside the garden. The house was big and dark, and gave one a cold feeling. Thaddeus pointed up at Bartholomew's window, but there was no light.

Holmes said, "But I see a little light in the window beside the door."

"Ah, that is the housekeeper's room.

That's where old Mrs. Bernstone stays. But perhaps you should wait here for a minute or two, because if we all go in together, she may be surprised. But, quiet! What is that?"

Thaddeus held up the light. From the great black house there sounded through the silent night the saddest of sounds—the crying of a frightened woman. Thaddeus hurried to the door, which was opened by an old woman.

"Oh, Mr. Thaddeus, sir, I am so glad you have come!" He went inside with her.

Holmes had the lantern now and was swinging it around, looking at the house and at the big piles of dirt in the garden.

Mary and I were both very frightened and stood there holding hands. Though I was frightened, I thought how romantic it was.

"What a strange place!" said Mary. "It

looks as though all the moles in England have been here."

"These are the holes of the treasure-seekers," said Holmes. "You must remember that they looked for it for six years."

At that moment, Thaddeus came rushing out of the house. "There is something wrong with Bartholomew!" he cried. "Oh, I am frightened!" He looked like a terrified child.

"Come into the house," said Holmes in his firm way. We all went inside and into the housekeeper's room. She also looked scared, but was calmed when she saw Mary's face.

"Master has locked himself in and will not answer me," explained the old lady. "I waited for him all day, and then about an hour ago I feared something might be wrong so I went up and looked through the keyhole. It was horrible! You must go up and see for yourself."

Holmes took the lamp and led the way. Thaddeus was shaking violently. Mary stayed below with the frightened housekeeper.

Up on the third floor, Holmes knocked on

Bartholomew's door, but there was no answer. He tried to open the door, but it was locked on the inside. He looked through the keyhole and stood up with a sharp intake of breath.

"There is something devilish in this, Watson," he said, more emotional than I had ever seen him. "What do you think?"

I also looked and jumped back in horror. Looking straight at me and floating in the air, for all beneath was in shadow, hung a face—the very face of our companion, Thaddeus. The face was set in a horrible smile, fixed and unnatural, more frightening than an angry face. The face was so like our bald friend that I had to turn around to make sure he was still with us. I then remembered that he and his brother were twins.

We broke open the door and went inside Bartholomew's room. It looked like a chemical laboratory. One of the containers had broken and the air had a strange smell. By the table in a wooden chair sat the master of the house with that smile on his face. He was stiff and

cold and clearly had been dead for many hours.

By his hand on the table there was a torn sheet of paper with the words 'The sign of the four' written on it.

"My God, what does it all mean?" I asked.

"It means murder," said Holmes, bending over the dead man. "Ah! I expected it. Look here!" He pointed to what looked like a long dark thorn stuck in the skin just above the ear.

"It looks like a thorn," I said.

"It is a thorn. You may take it out, but be careful because it is poisoned."

To me, the mystery was growing darker

and darker, but to Holmes it was getting clearer and clearer. He needed only a few missing links to have an entirely connected case.

We had almost forgotten about Thaddeus. He was standing in the doorway in horror.

Suddenly he cried out, "The treasure is gone! They have robbed him of the treasure. There is the hole in the ceiling through which we lowered it last night. I helped him do it! I was the last person who saw him. I left him here last night, and I heard him lock the door as I came downstairs."

"What time was that?" asked Holmes.

"It was ten o'clock. And now he is dead, and the police will be called in, and they will think that I did it. Oh, yes, I'm sure of it. But you don't think so, do you gentlemen? Surely you don't think that it was I? Oh, dear! Oh, dear! I know that I will go crazy!"

"You have no reason for fear, Mr. Sholto," said Holmes kindly, putting his hand upon his shoulder. "Take my advice and drive down to the station to report the matter to the police. Offer to assist them in every way. We shall wait here until your return."

He nodded in agreement and went down the stairs slowly, as if he were drunk.

Chapter 6

Sherlock Holmes
Gives a Demonstration

"Now, Watson," said Holmes, rubbing his hands. "We have half an hour to ourselves. Let us make good use of it. Simple as the case seems now, there may be something deeper underlying it."

"Simple?" I cried.

"Yes. In the first place, how did these people come and how did they go? The door has not been opened since last night. How about the window?"

He walked across to it, talking to himself rather than to me. The window was locked on the inside, there was no water pipe to climb up on the outside of the building, and the roof was out of reach. But a man climbed up to the window. There was a footprint on the edge and also a round muddy mark, and the same marks were on the floor and by the table.

"That round mark is not a footmark," I said.

"No, it is something much more valuable to us. It is the mark of a wooden stump."

"From a wooden-legged man."

"Yes. But there has been someone else—a very able helper. Could you climb that wall, Watson?"

I looked out of the open window. It was about 60 feet (18 meters) from the ground and there were no footholds for climbing. "It would be impossible," I said.

"But if you had a friend up here who lowered you this strong rope which I see in the corner, tying one end to this big hook in the wall, then maybe you could, even with a wooden leg. You could leave in the same way.

Your friend would pull up the rope, untie it from the hook, shut the window and lock it on the inside, and leave the way that he came. The wooden-legged man, however, was not accustomed to climbing with ropes. I see more than one blood mark on the rope, telling me he slipped down with such speed that he took the skin off his hands."

"But how did the mysterious friend come into the room?" I asked.

"Ah, yes, the friend. He is interesting and he makes this an unusual case."

Holmes thought it must have been through the hole in the roof, where the treasure was

hidden. We went up a ladder and into the secret room. It was very small. We found a trapdoor which led out onto the roof. This is how the helper entered. Holmes looked at the dusty floor of the room and saw the prints of a shoeless foot but it was only half the size of an ordinary man.

"Has a child done this terrible thing?" I asked, confused. Holmes did not answer, but went down again to the lower room and continued to look for clues.

"We are in luck," he said. "We ought to have very little trouble now. The helper stepped in the creosote and you can see the outline of his small foot here. We have got him now because I know a dog that would follow that smell to the end of the world. Ah, but wait, the police have arrived."

"Before they come up," said Holmes, "just put your hand here on this poor fellow's arm, and here on his leg. What do you feel?"

"The muscles are as hard as a board," I answered.

"Quite so, much harder than usual. What does it suggest to your mind?"

"Death from some very powerful poison."

"That's what I thought when I saw the face, and as you saw I found a thorn which had been driven or shot into the head. Now look at this thorn."

I looked closely at the thorn. It was long, sharp and black. Near the point it looked as though something sticky had dried upon it. The opposite end had been cut and rounded off with a knife.

"Is that an English thorn?" I asked.

"No, it certainly is not."

Just then the police came into the room. One of the policemen, Detective Athelney Jones, remembered Sherlock Holmes from a previous case. Holmes had, as usual, used theories to solve the case, but the policeman thought his success was only good luck.

"But what is all this?" said Jones. "Bad, bad. Now let's have the facts—no room for theories. What do you think this man died of?"

"Oh, I'm sure you don't want any of my theories, detective," said Holmes dryly.

"No, no. Still, we can't deny that you are exactly right sometimes. Oh, dear. Door locked. I understand jewels worth half a million missing. How was the window?"

"Locked, but there are footprints on the sill."

"Well, well, if it was locked the footprints could have nothing to do with the matter. That's common sense. The man might have died from shock; but then the jewels are missing. Ha! I have a theory. These flashes come upon me at times. Sholto was, by his own confession, with his brother last night. He killed his brother in anger and then walked off with the treasure. How's that?"

"On which the dead man very kindly got up and locked the door on the inside," Holmes said jokingly.

"Hmm, I see your point. Let us use common sense. Thaddeus was with his brother. There was a fight. This we know. The brother is dead and the jewels are gone. This we also know. No one saw the brother from the time Thaddeus left him. His bed had not been slept in. Thaddeus is in a troubled state of mind. You see that I am making a case against Thaddeus."

"You do not yet have all the facts," said Holmes. "This thorn, which I think was poisoned, was in the man's head, where you still see the mark. This piece of paper with the writing on it was on the table. How does all that fit into your theory?"

"Confirms it in every way," said the man confidently. "If this thorn is poisonous, Thaddeus may as well have used it as any other man. The paper is some kind of trick, to lead us away from the facts. The only question is how did he leave? Ah, of course, here is a hole in the roof."

He went up to examine the secret room, found the trapdoor and came down to say that facts are better than theories and that his view of the case was confirmed. He called for Thaddeus to come into the room.

"Mr. Sholto, it is my duty to inform you that anything which you may say will be used against you. I arrest you in the Queen's name as being concerned in the death of your brother."

"You see? Didn't I tell you?" cried the poor little man, throwing up his hands and looking from one to the other of us.

"Don't worry, Mr. Sholto," said Holmes. "I think I can clear you of the charge."

"Don't promise too much, Mr. Theorist!" said Jones in an angry voice.

"Not only will I clear him, sir, but I will tell you the name and description of one of the two people who were in this room last night. His name is Jonathan Small and he's

got a wooden leg which is worn away on the inner side. He is a middle-aged man, very sunburned, and he has been in jail before. These few things may help you, together with the fact that there is a lot of skin missing from the palm of his hand."

The policeman was not happy that Holmes knew all these things because he wanted to be the clever one, but he listened carefully.

"The other man is a rather strange person," continued Holmes. "I hope to be able to introduce you to both of them soon."

At this point Holmes took me out in the hall and asked me to take Miss Morstan home and then return. He also wanted me to drop by a friend's place to pick up a dog named Toby, and bring him back with me.

"Toby has an amazing sense of smell and can surely lead us to the killers. I would rather have Toby's help than the whole detective force of London."

It was 1:00 in the morning and I hoped to be back by 3:00. In the meantime, Holmes would question Mrs. Bernstone and Bartholomew's Indian servant, Lal Rao.

Chapter 7
The Episode of the Barrel

The police had brought a cab with them and I took Miss Morstan home in it. She had been calm until now, but in the cab she started crying because of the adventures of the night. I wanted to do something. I wanted to speak my words of affection, but two thoughts stopped me. She was weak and helpless that night and it would have been wrong to show my love at such a time. Worse still, she was rich and she might look upon me as a mere fortune seeker. I dropped Miss Morstan off at her home and made my way over to get Toby.

On the way I thought about everything that

had happened and how wild and dark it all was to me. There was the original problem: the death of Captain Morstan, the sending of the pearls, the ad in the newspaper, the letter—we had some light upon all those events. They had only led us, however, to a deeper mystery. The Indian treasure, the curious paper found among Morstan's things, the strange scene at Major Sholto's death, the rediscovery of the treasure immediately followed by the murder of the discoverer, the things connected with the crime—the footsteps, the strange thorn, the words upon the piece of paper which were the same as those on Captain Morstan's paper. I thought that only a man like Holmes could begin to understand these things.

I found the house where Toby's owner lived and asked to borrow the dog for a short time. The owner was a friend of Holmes's and agreed

quickly. Toby was an ugly, long-haired dog, with ears that hung down loosely, a mixed breed, brown and white in color and walked like a duck. We got back to Pondicherry Lodge at three in the morning. I found that Thaddeus, the gatekeeper, the housekeeper and the Indian servant had been taken to the police station, all under arrest.

Holmes said he wanted to check something on the roof. I waited in the garden with Toby while he followed a path where the tiles of the roof had come loose. This took him to a corner where there was a water pipe going up the wall. It looked strong and he came down to the ground on this pipe. He showed me what he had found on the roof – something which looked like a cigarette case. Inside this case were six sharp pieces of wood, the thorns like that which had struck Bartholomew. This was good news because if we found the killer, we didn't want him to shoot any poison thorns at us.

"Are you ready for a long walk, Watson?"

THE SIGN OF THE FOUR

I said yes and Holmes put a handkerchief he had dipped in creosote under Toby's nose. He then threw the handkerchief far off and tied a rope to the dog's neck, leading him to the place where he had come down the water pipe.

Toby instantly started barking, and with his nose on the ground and his tail in the air, ran off at a fast pace.

It was starting to get light. Toby reached the wall of the garden, ran along it and finally stopped in a corner. Holmes climbed the wall, took the dog and dropped it over the other side. We found a little blood on the white wall and thought it was the handprint of the man with the wooden leg.

The creosote clue was just one of the ways Holmes could trace the criminals, but it was the strongest. But to me it was all still very mysterious and I asked Holmes how he could have described the wooden-legged man with such confidence.

"It was very simple. Two officers, Captain

Morstan and Major Sholto, who are in command of a prison learn an important secret as to buried treasure. A map is drawn for them by an Englishman named Jonathan Small. You remember that we saw the name on the map which Captain Morstan had. He had signed it on behalf of himself and his associates—the sign of the four, as he called it. Aided by this map, the officers, or one of them, gets the treasure and brings it to England. But probably he got it without keeping some promise. Why didn't Jonathan Small get the treasure himself? Jonathan Small did not get the treasure because he and his associates were themselves in prison and could not get away."

"But you must be just guessing," I said.

"It is more than that. It is the only idea which covers the facts. Let us see how it fits with what follows. Major Sholto remains at peace for some years, happy with his treasure. Then he receives a letter from India, which frightens him. What was that?"

"A letter to say that the men whom he had

wronged had been set free."

"Or had escaped. What does he do then? He guards himself against a man he believes is coming for his treasure. Now, from Jonathan Small's point of view, he came to England with two purposes in mind—to get his part of the treasure and to get revenge on the man who wronged him. He finds out where Sholto lives but he does not know where the treasure was hidden. Suddenly, Small learns that Major Sholto is about to die, so he rushes to the house and appears at the window but does not enter because his two sons are with him. Crazy with hate, however, he enters the room that night, searches his private papers in hopes of finding information about the treasure and finally leaves the message on the piece of paper we found. Later he finds out about the secret room from someone inside the house. Small, with his wooden leg, cannot possibly reach the third floor and get into Bartholomew's room, so he takes another person with him—the one who steps in the creosote."

"So it was the other person and not Small who did the crime."

"Yes. But Small did not wish for Bartholomew to die. It happened because of the wild character of his companion and the poison did its work so quickly. Small then lowered the treasure box to the ground and came down off the roof himself. As to his personal appearance, he must be middle-aged and must be sunburned after being in prison in such a hot place as the Andamans. His height is easily known from the length of his step."

We had during this time been following Toby down the roads which led to the city. It was getting lighter and people were beginning to appear. Toby paid no attention to them and kept his nose to the ground, barking from time to time, which meant he was getting closer to the goal. At one point Toby stopped, turned backwards showing doubt and looked up to Holmes and me, as if to ask for sympathy for not knowing what to do.

"What's the matter with the dog?" said Holmes.

"Perhaps they stood here for some time," I suggested.

"Ah, it's all right! He's off again," said Holmes.

Toby was indeed off. After smelling again, he suddenly made up his mind and ran with an energy and determination which he had not yet shown. He did not now need to put his nose to the ground. By the look in Holmes's eyes, I thought we were getting near the end of the journey.

We had come to a large lumber yard. Here the dog was very excited and went in through the gate, raced through the yard, went between two wood piles and finally, with a loud bark, jumped at a large container. With his tongue hanging out and his eyes blinking, Toby stood there looking from one to the other of us for some kind of thanks. The container had the color and strong smell of creosote. Toby had brought us to one of the many construction yards that use creosote. We looked at each other and then burst into laughter.

Chapter 8
The Baker Street Irregulars

"What do we do now?" I asked. "We can see that Toby is not quite perfect."

"Well, there is a lot of creosote carried around London. Poor Toby is not to blame."

"We must get on the main track again, I suppose."

"Yes, and luckily we have not far to go. It seems that what puzzled the dog back there was that there were two different trails going in opposite directions. We took the wrong one. It only remains to follow the other."

We went back to the place where Toby had gotten confused. He went around in a wide circle and finally ran off in a new direction. It seemed that we were on the real path now. We went down towards the riverside and finally to the water's edge, where there was a small wooden wharf. Toby took us to the very edge of this and stood there crying, looking out on the dark water beyond.

"We are out of luck," said Holmes. "They have taken a boat from here."

Nearby was a small house with a sign on it reading 'Boats to hire by the hour or day.'

We went to the house and spoke to the woman inside, a Mrs. Smith. Holmes asked for her husband, but was told he had been away since the morning of the day before and that she was feeling frightened about him.

He had gone off in the steamboat, but without much fuel. She went on to say she didn't like that wooden-legged man who went with him. She described him as a brown, monkey-faced man who had come to see her husband more than once. He had come about 3:00 in the morning and her husband had known that he was coming.

She knew it was the wooden-legged man by his voice. Her husband and her eldest son, Jim, went away with him in the boat. She wasn't sure if the wooden-legged man had come alone. Holmes got a description of the boat from the woman—the name, the color and so on. It was called the Aurora.

We wondered what to do next, how to proceed and look for the men. There were so many places along the river to look. It would take a very long time to check every possibility.

We did not want to tell the police how far we had come or ask people along the river. We were afraid this would make the men aware they were being chased. If they did not think anyone was looking for them, they would feel safe and not be in a hurry to go anywhere, like a foreign country.

We decided to go home, have some breakfast and get an hour's sleep. We kept Toby, thinking he might still be of use to us. Holmes stopped by a post office on the way to send a telegraph.

It was now between eight and nine o'clock in the morning and I was feeling weak in mind and body. I had a bath and changed my clothes, while Holmes prepared breakfast. The morning paper had an article about the murder. It reported that the most clever mind of the police force, Jones, had solved the crime and had arrested four people. There was more praise for the police officer than information about the case.

Holmes laughed about the article, but I said we were lucky not to have been arrested ourselves! At that moment the doorbell rang and we could hear a lot of noise downstairs. I again wondered if we would now be arrested.

"No, it's not quite so bad as that," Holmes

THE SIGN OF THE FOUR

said. "It is the unofficial force—the Baker Street irregulars." In came 12 dirty and ragged little street children.

"Got your telegram, sir," said the one called Wiggins, "and brought everyone quickly."

Holmes paid them for the money they had spent to come. He told them that he wanted to find the steamboat called the Aurora and described what it looked like. He wanted the group to search both sides of the river. One person was to go and wait near the Smith house. He gave them some money in advance and they were on their way.

"Are you going to bed, Holmes?" I asked.

"No, I'm not tired. I'm rather strange. I never remember feeling tired by work, though doing nothing makes me very tired. I am going to smoke and to think over this strange business. This ought to be an easy job. Wooden-legged men are not so common, but the other man must be very unique."

"That other man again!"

"Yes, you must have formed your own opinion of him—very small feet, able to move very quickly, small poisoned thorns—what do you think?"

"A wild man!" I said.

"Perhaps. The little thorns could only be shot in one way. They are from a blowpipe. Now, then, where are we to find our wild man?"

"South America," I guessed.

"I think not," said Holmes as he took a big book from the shelf.

He found the entry for the Andaman Islands and the people who live there. The book said they may be the smallest race upon this earth. They are a very wild people but able to have close friendships when their confidence has been gained. Among other features, their feet and hands are extremely small. They shoot poisoned thorns when facing their enemies.

I was very tired. Holmes told me to lie down on the sofa and he would put me to sleep by playing the violin. I soon found myself in dreamland, with the sweet face of Mary Morstan looking down upon me.

Chapter 9
A Break in the Chain

It was late in the afternoon before I woke, strengthened and refreshed. Sherlock Holmes still sat exactly as I had left him, except that he had laid aside his violin and was deep in a book. He looked across at me as I moved, and I noticed that his face was dark and troubled.

"You have slept well," he said. "I feared that our talk would wake you."

"I heard nothing," I answered. "Have you had fresh news, then?"

"Unfortunately, no. I must say that I am surprised and disappointed. Wiggins has just come to report. He says that no trace can be found of the boat. It bothers me because every hour is important."

"Can I do anything? I am perfectly fresh now, and quite ready for another adventure tonight."

"No, we can do nothing. We can only wait. If we go ourselves, a message might come in our absence and that would cause a delay. You are free to do what you wish, but I must remain on guard."

"Then shall I go over to see Miss Morstan? She asked me to, yesterday."

"Oh, Miss Morstan?" asked Holmes with a smile in his eyes.

"Well, yes. She was anxious to hear what had happened. I will be back in an hour or two," I said.

"All right! Good luck! But, if you are crossing the river, you may as well return Toby, for I do not think that we shall have any use for him now."

I took the dog back and paid the owner for the use of him. When I reached Miss

Morstan's place I found her a little tired from the previous night, but she wanted to hear the news. Mrs. Forrester, the landlady, was also very interested. I told them all that they had done.

"It's a romance!" cried Mrs. Forrester. "An injured lady, a half million in treasure, a black wild man and a wooden-legged criminal."

"And two heroes to the rescue," added Miss Morstan, looking at me with a bright face.

"Mary, I don't think that you are nearly excited enough. Just imagine what it must be to be so rich. You could do anything," Mrs. Forrester said.

"I am only worried about Mr. Thaddeus Sholto," Mary said. "Nothing else is important. He has been very brave and honorable from the beginning. We must help clear him."

I was happy to notice that Mary was not interested in becoming rich. It was evening before I left the two ladies, and quite dark by the time I reached home.

Holmes's book and pipe lay by his chair but he had disappeared. I asked our landlady Mrs. Hudson about him.

"Well, after walking up and down, up and down in the study, he finally went to his room. I'm quite worried about his health."

"I don't think you need to worry," I told her. "I have seen him like this before. He has some small matter on his mind which makes him restless."

I tried to speak lightly to the landlady but I myself was somewhat uneasy when through the long night I still heard from time to time the sound of his footsteps. I knew how Holmes was struggling against not being able to take any action.

At breakfast he looked very tired and as though he had a slight fever. "You are making yourself too tired," I said. "I heard you walking around in the night."

"I could not sleep," he answered. "This problem is burning me up. It is too much to be stopped by such a small thing; everything else has gone well. I know about the men, the boat, everything! The whole river has been searched on both sides, but there is no news, nor has Mrs. Smith heard from her husband."

"Perhaps Mrs. Smith gave us the wrong information."

"No, I don't think so. I asked around and there is a boat of that description."

"Could they have gone up the river?"

"I have thought about that, too, and there is a search party who will work up as far as Richmond. If no news comes today, I will go off myself tomorrow and look for the men rather than the boat. But, surely, surely, we will hear something."

We did not, however. Not a word came to us either from Wiggins or from other people. There were articles in most of the newspapers about the murder. They all seemed to be against poor Thaddeus

Sholto. There were no fresh details in any of them, except that a hearing was to be held on the following day.

I went to see Mary and Mrs. Forrester again that evening and on my return I found Holmes to be very depressed and quiet. He would hardly talk. He did not sleep again that night.

Early in the morning I woke with a start and was surprised to find Holmes standing by my bedside.

"I am going down the river," he said. "I have thought about everything and can see only one way. It is worth trying."

"Surely I should go with you!" I said.

"I don't want you to go because it's quite possible that some message may come during the day. I want you to open all notes and telegrams and use your own judgment if any news should come. Can I rely on you?"

"Most certainly."

"I may not be gone very long and I will have some sort of news before I get back."

That morning there was some fresh news in the paper. It had been shown that Thaddeus and the housekeeper, Mrs. Bernstone, were not involved in the murder and had been released. The police now had a clue as to the real criminals and the case was being checked further. For me it was good to know that Sholto was safe and I wondered what the new clue may be. It was, I thought, just a cover-up for the mistake the police had made.

It was a long day. Every time that a knock came to the door or a person passed in the street, I thought it might be Holmes or one of the children. At three o'clock I was surprised to be paid a visit by Detective Jones, the one who had arrested Thaddeus Sholto. He was not now the master of common sense that we had met before. He was no longer so confident. His expression was sad, like he was sorry for something.

I invited him in and offered him a cigar and a glass of whisky. Jones accepted, with thanks. I told him that Holmes had gone out.

He nodded his head. "You know my theory about this case?" he said.

"I remember that you said something."

"Well, I have to reconsider it. I thought it was Sholto who did it but there was a hole in my net. He was able to prove where he was at the time of the murder. It is very bad to be wrong and I need a little help."

"We all need help, sometimes," I said.

"Your friend, Mr. Sherlock Holmes, is a wonderful man. He's a man who cannot be defeated. I have seen him go into many cases and he has always been able to make things clear. He sent me a telegram saying that he has got some clue to the case."

Jones handed the message to me and it read:

Go to Baker Street at once. If I have not returned, wait for me. I am close on the track of the Sholto gang. You can come with us tonight if you want to be there at the finish.

"This sounds good. It looks like he is on the trail again," I said.

"I don't think so. Even the best of us make mistakes sometimes. But it is my duty not to miss any chances. Ah, there is someone at the door."

It was an old man, wearing the same kind of clothes that Holmes was wearing when he went out. His back was bent, his knees were shaking and his breathing was rough. He had a scarf around his chin and little of his face could be seen. He had dark eyes and hairy eyebrows and long, gray sideburns. He looked like an old sailor.

The old man asked for Mr. Sherlock Holmes.

"He is not here now but I am acting for him and you can give me your message. Is it about the Smith boat?"

"Yes, I know where it is. I know where the men are. And I know where the treasure is. I know all about it."

"Then tell me and I will let him know."

"I should tell Mr. Holmes."

"Well you must wait for him."

"No, no. I can't stay here and wait. If Mr. Holmes isn't here, then he'll have to find out about it by himself. I don't like the looks of you two and I won't say a word."

The old man went toward the door but Jones got in front of him.

"Wait a while, my friend," he said. "You have important information and you must not go away. We will keep you here until Holmes returns."

"Some treatment this is!" he said. "I come here to see a gentleman and you two, who I never saw in my life, treat me in this way." The old man finally sat down and Jones and I continued talking. Suddenly, however, Holmes's voice broke in upon us.

The old man was gone but Holmes was there. "Holmes!" I exclaimed. "You are here! But where is the old man?"

"Here is the old man," he said, holding out some white hair. "I thought my disguise was

pretty good, but I didn't think I could fool you."

Jones and I were delighted by the performance. Holmes explained that he had been working in the disguise all day because some members of the criminal world might recognize him.

"You got my telegram?" asked Holmes.

"Yes, that is what brought me here," said Jones.

"Now, Jones, you must do as I say. You can take all the credit, but you must act on the lines that I point out. Is that agreed?"

"Entirely, if you will help me find the men."

"All right, in the first place, I want a fast police-boat to be at the Westminster Stairs at 7:00."

"That is easy."

"Then I want two strong men in case of resistance."

"There will be two or three in the boat. What else?"

"When we find the men, we will find the treasure." Pointing to me, Holmes continued, "I think my friend here would like to take it first to the young lady to whom half of it belongs. Let her be the first to open it. Eh, Watson?"

"It would be a great pleasure," I agreed.

Jones said the treasure would afterwards have to be taken to the police station until the case was closed.

"One other point," said Holmes. "I would like to talk to Jonathan Small himself. May I have an unofficial interview if he is well guarded?"

Jones agreed.

"Is there anything else?" asked Jones.

"Yes, please have dinner with us."

Chapter 10
The End of the Islander

Holmes was in a good mood during dinner, and Jones and I also were feeling merry, mostly because we thought we were coming to the end of our task.

Holmes looked at his watch after the meal. He filled three more glasses with wine and said, "To the success of our journey. And now it is time to go. Do you have your gun, Watson?"

"It's in my desk."

"You had better take it, then. It is good to be prepared. I see that the taxi is at the door. I ordered it for 6:30."

It was a little past 7:00 when we reached Westminster Stairs and found the police boat waiting for us. There were four other men on the boat.

"Where to?" asked Jones.

"To the Tower. Tell them to stop opposite Jacobson's Yard."

I asked Holmes how he knew where to go.

"I put myself in the position of Jonathan Small. He would need the boat for his escape, somewhere nearby, but he could not leave it on the river because it might be found if the police were looking for the boat. I thought the only way to have both things was to put it in a repair yard. It would be hidden and yet available at short notice."

Holmes had disguised himself as a sailor and asked at all the yards down the river. He had no luck at 15 yards but at the 16th—Jacobson's—he learned that the Aurora had been handed over to them two days ago by a wooden-legged man, telling them to do something about the rudder.

Holmes put a guardman on the boat, who was to stand at the water's edge and wave his handkerchief when Small was getting on the boat. Holmes thought we would be able to take the men, the treasure and all.

We waited and waited and finally saw a white handkerchief moving. And then we saw the Aurora, moving very fast.

Jones looked worried and shook his head. He didn't think we could catch them. We increased our speed to the maximum. The Aurora sped on and we followed closely on her track.

"Faster, faster!" cried Holmes.

"I think we're gaining a little," said Jones with his eyes on the Aurora.

Just then another boat came between us and almost caused an accident. This allowed the Aurora to pull ahead by about 200 yards (180 meters). But we could still see her clearly. We followed every move of the boat ahead, and when we turned on the spotlight we could see the men on the deck.

The men on the Aurora now knew without a doubt that they were being chased and they tried to increase their speed.

We were gaining again. This was the most thrilling chase that I had ever experienced. Closer and closer we came. Jones yelled to them to stop. We were not more than four boat-lengths behind.

A man on the back end of the Aurora stood up and shook his fists at us, cursing in a cracked voice. It was Jonathan Small, a powerful-looking man. There was also a little black man on the deck, the smallest I had ever seen, with a big, oddly shaped head. His face looked like a cruel beast. We took out our guns.

"Shoot if he raises his hand," Holmes told me.

We were within a boat-length by this time

and almost within reach of our target. It was good that we had so clear a view of the small black man, the islander. As we looked at him, he took out a short, round piece of wood and put it between his teeth. We  shot at the same time, Holmes and I, and the man fell dead into the river.

Just then, the wooden-legged man turned his boat sharply toward the shore. Jones's men also turned quickly, but by then the Aurora was almost at the shore. With a bumping noise, it ran into the mud on the shore. Small jumped off the boat, but his wooden leg sank down into the muddy soil and he could not move no matter how much he tried, not forward, not backward. The more he moved, the deeper his wooden leg sank.

We came near him and threw the end of a

rope over his shoulders. We were then able to pull him out and drag him over the side of our boat.

The two Smiths, father and son, sat on the Aurora, but came on our boat when ordered to do so. The Aurora herself we tied to the back of our boat.

A solid iron chest of Indian workmanship stood upon the deck. This, there could be no question, was the same that had contained the treasure of the Sholtos. There was no key, but it was very heavy, so we took it carefully to our cabin. As we went slowly up the river again, we flashed the searchlight in every direction, but there was no sign of the little black man.

Chapter 11
The Great Agra Treasure

Our prisoner sat in the cabin opposite the iron box which he had done so much for and waited so long to gain. He was a sunburned man with frightening eyes. He had many lines and wrinkles on his face, which showed that he had had a hard, open-air life. He looked to be about 50 years old. He sat now with his handcuffed hands upon his legs and his head hanging down, while he looked at the box.

It seemed to me that there was more sorrow than anger in his face. He even once looked up with an expression of humor in his eyes.

"Well, Jonathan Small," said Holmes, lighting a cigar, "I am sorry that it has come to this."

"And so am I, sir," he answered frankly. "But I never did anything against Mr. Sholto. It was that little black devil, Tonga, who shot one of his thorns into him. I had no part in it, sir. I was as sad as if it had been my blood-relation. I beat the little devil with the end of a rope for it, but I could not undo it again."

"Have a cigar," said Holmes, "and you had better take a drink from my bottle because you are wet. How could you expect such a small man as Tonga to overpower Mr. Sholto and hold him while you were climbing the rope?"

"You seem to know as much about it as if you were there, sir. The truth is that I hoped to find the room empty. I knew the habits of the house pretty well, and it was the time when Mr. Sholto usually went downstairs for dinner. With Bartholomew Sholto I had no problem at all, so I had no intention of harming him."

"You are in the hands of Mr. Jones. He is going to bring you to my place and I will ask you to tell us the whole story. You must be completely truthful. If you are, I may be able to help you. I think that I can prove that the poison acts so quickly that the man was dead before you even reached the room."

"Yes, he was already dead, sir. I was never so surprised in my life as when I saw him smiling at me with his head on his shoulder as I climbed through the window. It really shook me. The truth is," he added with a bitter smile, "it was a bad day for me when I first saw the merchant Achmet and got mixed up with the Agra treasure, which never brought anything but evil to the man who had it. To Achmet it brought murder, to Major Sholto it brought fear and guilt, and to me it has meant prison for life."

At this moment Jones came into the tiny cabin.

"Well, I think we may all congratulate each other," he said. "Pity we didn't take the other alive but there was no choice. It was just lucky that we could overtake the Aurora."

"All's well that ends well," said Holmes.

"We will soon be landing," said Jones, "and we shall put you ashore, Dr. Watson, with the treasure box. But this is most irregular and, as a matter of duty, I must send a police officer with you, since you will have such a valuable thing. It is a pity there is no key, so that we could see what's inside first. You will have to break it open. Where is the key, my man?"

"At the bottom of the river," said Small.

"Why did you give us this extra trouble? We have had enough work already because of you. Anyway, Dr. Watson, be careful. Bring the box back with you to the Baker Street rooms."

They put me, the police officer and the box

ashore. A quarter of an hour's drive took us to Mrs. Forrester's place. The servant told us that Mrs. Forrester was out, but that Miss Morstan was inside. The police officer waited in the cab while I went in with the box.

Mary was seated by the open window. When she heard me come in, she jumped to her feet and smiled with surprise and pleasure.

"I heard a cab drive up," she said. "I thought that Mrs. Forrester had come back very early but I never dreamed that it might be you. What news have you brought me?"

"I have brought something better than news," I said, putting down the box upon the table and looking at her joyfully, even though my heart was heavy within me. "I have brought you something which is worth all the news in the world. I have brought you a fortune."

She looked at the iron box. "Is that the treasure, then?" she asked, coolly enough.

"Yes, this is the great Agra treasure. Half of it is yours and half is Thaddeus Sholto's. You will be one of the richest young ladies in

England. Isn't it glorious?"

I thought that she noticed an empty ring in my congratulations because I saw her eyebrows rise a little and she looked at me in a strange way.

"All I have," she said, "I owe to you."

"No, no." I answered, "not to me but to my friend, Sherlock Holmes. With all the will in the world, I could never have followed up a clue which was difficult even for him. As it was, we very nearly lost the thieves at the last moment."

"Please sit down and tell me about it, Dr. Watson," she said.

I told her briefly what had happened since I last saw her—Holmes's new method of search, the discovery of the Aurora, the joining with Jones, and the wild chase down the river. She listened with parted lips and shining eyes to my tale of adventure. When I spoke of the dart which had so narrowly missed us, she turned so white that I feared that she was about to faint.

"It is nothing," she said, as I hurried to pour her out some water. "I am all right again. It was a shock to me to hear that I had placed my friends in such horrible danger."

"That is all over," I answered. "It was nothing. I will tell you no more bad details. Let us turn to something brighter. There is the treasure. What could be brighter than that? I was allowed to bring it with me, thinking that it would interest you to be the first to see it."

"What a pretty box!" she said, bending over it. "This is Indian work, I suppose?"

"Yes, it is Benares metal-work."

"And so heavy," she exclaimed, trying to lift it. "The box alone must be of some value. Where is the key?"

"Small threw it into the river," I answered. "I must borrow Mrs. Forrester's poker." I forced open the lock and with trembling fingers opened the lid. We both stood looking in astonishment. The box was empty! Not one piece of metal or jewelry lay in it.

"The treasure is lost," said Miss Morstan calmly.

As I listened to the words and realized what they meant, a great shadow seemed to pass from my soul. I did not know how much this Agra treasure had weighed me down until now that it was finally removed. I thought it was selfish, disloyal, and wrong, but I could only think that now nothing separated us.

"Thank God!" I said from my very heart.

She looked at me with a quick, questioning smile. "Why do you say that?"

"Because you are within my reach again," I said, taking her hand. She did not withdraw it. "Because I love you,  Mary, as truly as ever a man loved a woman. Because this treasure, these riches, kept me quiet. Now that they are gone I can tell you how I love you. That is why I said, 'Thank God.'"

"Then I say 'Thank God,' too," she whispered as I drew her to my side.

Whoever had lost a treasure, I knew that night that I had gained one.

Chapter 12

The Strange Story of Jonathan Small

I went back to Baker Street, where Holmes, Jones and Small had only just arrived. When I showed them the empty box, Small leaned back in his chair and laughed aloud.

"This is your doing, Small," said Jones angrily.

"Yes, I have put it away where you will never find it. It is my treasure and if I can't have it, no one can. No living man has any right to it, unless it is three men who are in the Andaman prison, and myself. All the time I have acted for them as much as for myself. It's been the sign of the four with us always. Well, I know that they would have had me do just what I have done, and throw the treasure into the river rather than let it go to the family of Sholto or Morstan."

"You are lying to us, Small," said Jones; "if you had wished to throw the treasure into the river, it would have been easier for you to have thrown it box and all."

"Easier for me to throw and easier for you to find," he answered. "The man who was clever enough to hunt me down is clever enough to pick an iron box from the bottom of a river. Now that they are scattered over five miles (eight km) or so, it may be a harder job."

"This is a very serious matter, Small. If you had helped us, you would have had a better chance at your trial."

"Help?" Small said angrily. "What help should I give to those who have never earned it? Look how I have earned it! I spent 20 long years working hard under the hot sun, chained up at night like a dog, burning with fever, bullied by black policemen who loved to beat a white man. That was how I earned the Agra treasure."

Small had lost all of his control in this outburst of anger. I could understand the fear that Major Sholto had when he first learned that Small was on his track.

"You forget that we know nothing of all this," said Holmes quietly. "We have not heard your story and we cannot tell if perhaps justice may have been on your side at one time."

"Well, sir, if you want to hear my story, I have no wish to hold it back. What I say to you is God's truth, every word of it. I am from Worcestershire, born near Pershore. My family were all steady church-going folk, small farmers, well-known and respected, but I was always different. When I was about 18, I joined the army and went to India.

"I was not destined to be a soldier for long, however. I had just learned to march and handle my gun, when I was fool enough to go swimming in the Ganges. A crocodile took me just as I was halfway across and bit off my right leg as clean as a doctor could have done it, just above the knee. With the shock and the loss of blood, I fainted, and might have died if my sergeant had not caught hold of me and swam for the shore. I got this wooden leg and found myself out of the army and not suitable for any active job.

"I was down on my luck, and not yet 20 years old. However, my misfortune soon proved to be a blessing in disguise. A man named Abel White, who had come out there as an indigo-planter, wanted someone to look after his workers. Since most of the work was to be done on a horse, my leg was not a problem. I had to ride over the plantation to keep an eye on the men as they worked, and to report those who were not working. The pay was fair, I had a small but nice place to live and altogether I was happy to spend the rest of my life there.

"Well, I was never lucky for long. Suddenly, there was a great uprising against the British. One month India was peaceful and the next there were 200,000 black devils let loose and the country was a perfect hell.  I'm sure you read about it in the newspapers. My boss did not think it was so serious, so we didn't leave with the other Europeans on their way to Agra, the closest army fort.

"One day I was riding home from another plantation when I saw Abel White's house in flames. From where I stood I could see hundreds of black people, dancing and screaming around the burning house. Some of them pointed at me and a couple of bullets went past my head. So I ran away on the horse across the fields and found myself late at night safe within the walls of Agra.

"The old fort of Agra is a very strange, very big place. There is a modern part, which held all of us and the supplies, with plenty of room to spare. But the modern part is nothing like the size of the old quarter, where nobody goes, and which is full of poisonous insects. It is full of great deserted halls, and winding passages, so that it is easy enough for someone to get lost in it.

"The river flows along the front of the old fort, and so protects it, but on the sides and behind there are many doors and these had to be guarded, of course. We were short-handed, so it was impossible for us to post a strong guard at every one of the many gates. I was chosen to take charge of a small isolated door on the southwest side of the building. There were two Sikh soldiers under my command and I was told to fire my gun if anything went wrong.

"Well, I was pretty proud at having this small command, since I was so new to the army, and a wooden-legged man at that. For two nights I kept the watch with my two Sikhs. Their names were Mahomet Singh and Abdullah Khan and they were both tall and fierce-looking.

"The third night of my watch was dark and rainy. I took out my pipe and laid down my gun to strike a match. In an instant the Sikhs were upon me. One of them took my gun and pointed it at my head, while the other held a knife to my throat, saying that he would kill me if I moved a step.

"Mahomet said 'Don't make a noise. The fort is safe enough.' I waited in silence to see what it was that they wanted from me.

"'Listen to me,' said the one called Khan. 'You must either be with us now, or you must be silenced forever. The thing is too great a one for us to hesitate. Either you are heart and soul with us or your body will be thrown into the river. There is no middle way. Which is it to be — death or life?'

"'How can I decide?' I asked. 'You have not told me what you want of me.'

"Khan explained, 'We ask you to be rich. If you choose to help us, we promise that you will have your fair share of the treasure. A quarter of it will be yours.'

"'But what is the treasure, then?' I asked. 'I am as ready to be rich as you can be if you will show me how it can be done.'

"'Do you promise, then,' he said, 'to raise no hand and speak no word against us, either now, or afterwards?'

"'I promise,' I answered, 'only if the fort is not in danger.'

"'Then, my friend, I promise you that you will have one quarter of the treasure, which will be equally divided among the four of us.'

"'There are but three,' I said.

"'No. Dost Akbar must have his share. We can tell you the tale while we wait.'

"Then Khan told me a story that was hard to believe, but his eyes told me it was true, every word.

"'There is a rajah in the northern provinces who has much wealth, though his lands are small. Much has come to him from his father and more still he has made by himself. He keeps his gold rather than spending it.

"'Being a careful man, he made plans to keep his treasure safe. The most precious stones and the best pearls, he put in an iron box and sent by a trusted servant, posing as a merchant, to the fort at Agra, to be hidden there until India is at peace.

"'This so-called merchant whose name is Achmet, is traveling with my foster brother, Dost Akbar, who knows his secret. Dost Akbar has promised to lead him to a side gate of the fort, and has chosen this one for his purpose. He will come soon and here he will find Singh and myself waiting for him. The place is lonely and no one will know of his coming. Then the great treasure of the rajah will be divided among us. What do you say?'

"'I am with you heart and soul,' I said.

"'It is well,' he answered, handing me back my gun. 'You see that we trust you, because your word, like ours, is not to be broken. We have now only to wait for my brother and the merchant.'

"The rain was still falling steadily because it was just the beginning of the wet season. Brown, heavy clouds were going across the sky and it was hard to see very far. Suddenly I saw a light on the other side of the moat. It was coming slowly in our direction.

"'There they are!' I exclaimed.

"'You will stop him, as usual,' whispered Abdullah. 'Give him no cause for fear. Send us in with him and we shall do the rest while you stay here on guard.'

"The light kept coming, and I could see

two dark figures on the other side of the moat. I let them come down the sloping bank, splash through the mud, and climb halfway up to the gate before I challenged them.

"'Who goes there?' I called.

"'Friends,' came the answer. The first was a very big Sikh with a black beard which nearly came down to his waist-belt. The other was a little fat, round fellow with a great yellow turban and a bundle in his hand. He seemed to be shaking with fear and his head kept turning to left and right with two bright twinkling eyes.

"'I am so happy because I am once more safe—I and my poor things,' he said to me.

"'What have you in the bundle?' I asked.

"'An iron box,' he answered, 'which contains one or two little family matters, which are of no value to others but which I would be sorry to lose. I will reward you, young man, and your commander also if he will give me the shelter I ask.'

"'Take him to the main guard,' I said. The

two Sikhs closed in upon him on each side, and the giant walked behind, through the main gateway. I remained at the gateway with the lantern.

"I could hear their footsteps going through the lonely passages. Suddenly, they stopped and I heard voices and a struggle, with the sound of blows. A moment later there came, to my horror,  a rush of footsteps in my direction. I turned my lantern down the long passage, and there was the fat man, running like the wind. I put my gun between his legs as he raced past and he fell, then rolled twice over like a shot rabbit. Before he could get to his feet the Sikh was upon him and buried his knife in his side. The man did not cry out or move a muscle but lay where he had fallen."

Small stopped and held out his hands for the whisky and water which Holmes had made for him. To me this was a horrible man and whatever punishment he might get, he would get no sympathy from me.

"Go on with your story," said Holmes.

"Well, we carried him in, Khan, Akbar and I. Singh was left to guard the door. We took him to a place which the Sikhs had already prepared. The earth floor had sunk in at one place, making a natural grave, so we left Achmet the merchant there, having first covered him over with loose bricks. This done, we all went back to the treasure.

"It lay where he had dropped it when he was first attacked. The box was the same as that which now lies open upon your table. We opened it and the light of the lantern shined upon a collection of gems such as I have only dreamed of. It was blinding to look upon them. We took them all out and made a list of them. There were 143 diamonds, all first class, including one which has been called, I believe, 'the Great Mogul,' and is said to be the second largest stone in the world. Then there were 97 very fine emeralds and 170 rubies. Also, 210 sapphires, 61 agates, and a great quantity of other stones. Besides this, there were nearly 300 very fine pearls, 12 of which were set in a gold crown.

"We agreed to hide our treasure in a safe place until the country was at peace again, and then to divide it equally among ourselves. There was no use dividing it at that time, because if gems of such value were found on us, it would cause suspicion, and there was no place in the fort where we could keep them near us. We carried the box into the same hall where we had buried the body, and there, under certain bricks in the best-preserved wall, we made a hole and put our treasure in it. We made careful note of the place and the next day I drew four maps, one for each of us, and put the sign of the four of us at the bottom, because we had promised that we would each always act for all.

"Well, there's no use in telling you gentle-men what came of the Indian rebellion. It was broken by the English forces after a few months. Peace seemed to be settling upon the country, and we four were beginning to hope that we might safely go off with our shares of the treasure. However, our hopes were destroyed by our being arrested as the murder-ers of Achmet.

"It happened in this way. The rajah who sent Achmet with the box of jewels also sent a second person to follow him. This man saw Achmet go into the fort but never saw him come out. We were found guilty in court, though the treasure was never mentioned. because the rajah had left India and no one else knew about it. The murder, however, was clearly made out, and it was certain that we must all have played a part in it. We were to spend the rest of our lives in prison.

"So there we were all four in prison, with little chance of ever getting out again, while we each held a secret which could have made us richer than the richest of men. It might have driven me crazy, but I was always very stubborn so I did my best to endure the situation.

"At last my chance to escape seemed to have come. I and the three Sikhs were moved from Agra to Blair Island in the Andamans. There were very few white prisoners there and since I did nothing bad from the beginning, I soon found myself a kind of special person. I was given a small hut in Hope Town and I learned to pass out medicine for the doctor. I was even able to pick up a little of his knowledge. All the time I was on the lookout for a chance to escape; but the island was very far from any other land and there was little or no wind in those seas, so it was a very difficult job to get away.

"The doctor was a young man and he and the other young officers would meet in his rooms in the evening to play cards. The place where I worked to make the medicine was next to his sitting room, with a small window between us. I watched these games almost every night. Among the players were Major Sholto and Captain Morstan.

"Well, there was one thing which I soon noticed. The soldiers always used to lose and the civilians always used to win. Major Sholto was the hardest hit. He played for big sums and would sometimes win a few times, and then the bad luck would set in against him worse than ever. All day he would be in a black mood and began to drink more than was good for him.

"One night he lost even more heavily than usual. I was sitting in my hut when he and Captain Morstan were on the way to their rooms. They were very close friends, those two, always together. The major was shouting about his losses.

"'It's all over, Morstan,' he was saying as they passed my hut. 'I shall have to send in my papers to quit the army. I am a ruined man.'

"'Nonsense, old friend!' said the other, 'I've had a bad time myself, but—' That was all I could hear but it was enough to set me thinking.

"A couple of days later Major Sholto and Captain Morstan were walking on the beach so I took the chance to speak to them.

"'I wish to have your advice, please,' I started.

"'Well, Small, what is it?' Sholto asked.

"'I wanted to ask you, sir,' I continued, 'who is the proper person to whom a hidden treasure should be handed over? I know where half a million lies and, as I cannot use it myself, I thought the best thing would be to hand it over to the proper person and then perhaps he would get my sentence shortened for me.'

"'Half a million, Small?' he said with excitement, looking hard at me to see if I was telling the truth.

"'Yes, sir—in jewels and pearls. It lies there ready for anyone. And the strange thing about it is that the real owner has been forced out of India and cannot have it, so it belongs to whoever finds it first.'

"'To the government, Small, you mean it belongs to the government.' But he said this in a halting way and I knew in my heart that I had got him.

"'You think, then, sir, that I should give the information to the governor-general?' I asked.

"'Well, well, you must not do anything too quickly, or that you might be sorry for later. Let me hear all about it, Small. Give me the facts.'

"I told him the whole story, with small changes, so that he could not know the places. When I had finished, he stood very still and his face was full of thought.

"'This is a very important matter, Small,' he said at last. 'You must not say a word to anyone about it, and I shall see you again soon.'

"The next night, Sholto and Morstan came to see me in my hut.

"'Listen, Small,' said the major. 'We've been talking it over, my friend here and I, and we are sure that this secret of yours is not really a government matter, but is a private concern of your own. The question is, what price would you ask for it? We might be able to help, and at least look into it, if we could agree to something.' He tried  to speak in a cool, careless way, but his eyes were shining with excitement and greed.

"'Well, for that matter, gentlemen,' I answered, trying also to be cool but feeling as excited as he did, 'there is only one bargain which a man in my position can make. I shall want you to help me to my freedom, and to help my three friends to theirs. We shall then make you partners and give you a fifth share to divide between you.'

"'Oh,' he said. 'A fifth share! That is not very much.'

"'It would come to 50,000 each,' I said.

"'But how can we gain your freedom? You know very well that what you ask for is impossible.'

"'Not at all,' I answered. 'I have thought it all out to the last detail. The only thing stopping our escape is that we can get no boat for the trip, and no food to last us for so long a time. There are plenty of little boats at Calcutta or Madras which would be just fine. You bring one over. We will get on board at night, and if you will take us to any part of the Indian coast, you will have done your part.'

"'It would be so much better if there were only one person to escape,' he said.

"'None or all,' I answered. 'We have promised each other. The four of us must always act together.'

"'You see, Morstan,' Sholto said, 'Small is a man of his word. He does not go back on his friends. I think we may very well trust him.'

"'It's a dirty business,' the other answered, 'but I think you're right.'

"'Well, Small,' said the major, 'we must,

I suppose, try to help you. We must first, of
course, test the truth of your story. Tell me
where the box is hidden, and I will get time
off my job and go back to India in the monthly
supply-boat to check into things.'

"'Not so fast,' I said, growing colder as
he got hot. 'I must get the OK of my three
friends. I tell you that it is four or none with
us.'

"'Nonsense!' he broke in. 'What do three
black men have to do with our agreement?'

"'Black or blue,' I said, 'they are in with
me, and we all go together.'

"Well, the matter ended at a second meeting, at which Singh, Khan and Akbar were
all present. We talked the matter over again,
and at last we came to an agreement. We
were to give both officers a map of the part of
the Agra fort, and mark the place where the
treasure was hidden. Major Sholto was to go
to India to test our story. If he found the box,
he was to leave it there, to send out a small
boat supplied for a trip, which was to lie off

Rutland Island and to which we were to make our way, and finally to return to his duties. Captain Morstan was then to take time off duty, to meet us at Agra and there we were to have a final division of the treasure, he taking the major's share as well as his own.

"All this we sealed by the strongest promises that the mind could think of. I sat up all night with paper and ink, and by the morning, I had the two maps all ready, signed with the sign of the four—that is, of Abdullah, Dost, Mahomet and myself.

"Well, gentlemen, the evil Sholto went off to India, but he never came back again. He had stolen the treasure without keeping the promises on which we had sold him the secret. From that time I lived only for revenge. I thought of it all day and night. I cared nothing for the law—nothing for prison. To escape, to track down Sholto, to have my hand upon his throat—that was my one thought. Even the Agra treasure had come to be a smaller thing in my mind than the killing of Sholto.

"Well, I have set my mind on many things in this life, and never one which I did not carry out. But it was many years before my time came. I had told you that I had learned something of medicine. One day, when Dr. Somerton was down with a fever, a little Andaman Islander was picked up by some prisoners in the woods. He was sick to death and had gone to a lonely place to die. But I gave him some medicine and after a couple of months he got better and was able to walk. He took a liking to me then, and was always staying around my hut. I learned a little of his language from him, and this made him like me all the more.

"Tonga was his name. He was a very good boatman and owned a big canoe of his own. When I saw that he was so thankful and would do anything for me, I saw my chance of escape. I talked it over with him. He was to bring his boat around on a certain night to a place which was never guarded, and there he was to pick me up. I told him to bring lots of food and water.

"He was very true to me. No man ever had a better friend than Tonga. On the night we had named, he was waiting for me with his boat. I went to the boat and in an hour we were well out at sea. Tonga had brought all of his personal things with him. For 10 days we were at sea, trusting in luck and on the 11th we were picked up by a trading ship which was going from Singapore to Jiddah.

"Well, if I were to tell you all the adventures that my little friend and I went through, you would not thank me, because I would have you here until tomorrow morning. Here and there we went around the world, but something always kept us from going to London.

"All the time, however, I never forgot my purpose. I would dream of Sholto at night. I have killed him 100 times in my sleep. At last, however, some three or four years ago, we found ourselves in England. I had no great difficulty in finding where Sholto lived. I made friends with someone who could help me—I name no names because I don't want to get anyone else in trouble—and I soon found that he still had the jewels. Then I tried to get at him in many ways; but he was clever and, besides his sons, always had two bodyguards near him.

"One day, however, I got word that he was dying. I hurried at once to the garden, angry that he might slip out of my hands like that and, looking through the window, I could see he was close to death. I got into his room that same night, and I searched his papers to see if there was any record of where he had hidden our jewels. There was not a line and I came away as bitter as a man could be. Before I left I thought that if I ever met my Sikh friends again, they would be glad to know that I had left some mark of our hatred. So I wrote down the sign of the four of us, as it had been on the map and I put it on his chest.

"Then I heard that the treasure was being hunted for and, after some time, that it had been found. It was up at the top of the house in Mr. Bartholomew Sholto's chemical laboratory.

"I went at once and had a look at the place, but I could not see how, with my wooden leg, I could make my way up to it. I learned, however, about a trapdoor in the roof and also about Mr. Sholto's supper hour. It seemed to me that I could do it easily with Tonga's help. I took him with me and tied a long rope around his waist. He could climb like a cat and he soon made his way through the roof, but by bad luck, Bartholomew Sholto was still in the room. Tonga thought he had done something very clever in killing him.

"He was surprised when I got angry at him for killing the man. I took the treasure box and let it down, and then slid down myself, having first left the sign of the four upon the table to show that the jewels had come back at last to those who had most right to them. Tonga then pulled up the rope, closed the window and went out the way he had come in.

"I don't know if I have anything else to tell

you. All this is the truth, and if I tell it to you, gentlemen, it is not to amuse you, but it is only to let all the world know how badly I have myself been served by Major Sholto, and that I did not kill his son."

"A very interesting story," said Sherlock Holmes. "A suitable end to a very interesting case. There is nothing at all new to me in the last part of your story, except that you brought your own rope. That I did not know. By the way, I had hoped that Tonga had lost all his darts but he shot one at us in the boat."

"He had lost them all, sir, except the one which was in his blow-pipe at the time."

"Ah, of course," said Holmes. "I had not thought of that."

"Well, Holmes," said Jones, "I will feel more at ease when we have our storyteller here safe under lock and key. I thank you both for your help. Of course, you will be wanted at the trial. Good-night to you."

"Good-night, gentlemen," said Jonathan Small.

"Well, and there is the end of our little drama," I said, after Holmes and I had sat some time smoking in silence. "I fear it may be the last time I shall have the chance of studying your methods. Miss Morstan has done me the honor of accepting me as a husband."

Holmes groaned. "I feared as much. I really cannot congratulate you."

I was a little hurt. "Have you any reason to not like my choice?" he asked.

"Not at all. I think she is one of the most charming young ladies I have ever met. But love is an emotional thing and whatever is

emotional is opposed to that true cold reason which I place above all things. I would never marry myself because it would harm my reasoning power."

I laughed. "I think my reasoning will be all right. But you look very tired."

"Yes, I'm feeling it. I think I will be this way for a week."

"It all seems unfair," I said. "You have done all the work in this business, I get a wife out of it, Jones gets the credit, but what is there for you?"

"For me," said Sherlock Holmes, "there still remains the cocaine bottle." And he stretched his long white hand up for it.

Word List

A

☐ **a couple of** 2、3の

☐ **a lot of** たくさんの～

☐ **a matter of** ～の問題

☐ **a ~ or two** 1～か2～、2、3の

☐ **a sort of** ～のようなもの，一種の～

☐ **Abdullah Khan** アブドラ・カーン《人名》

☐ **Abel White** アベル・ホワイト《人名》

☐ **about** 熟 be about to まさに～しようとしている，～するところだ be worried about (～のことで)心配している，～が気になる[かかる] come about 起こる How about ~? ～はどうですか。～しませんか。worry about ～のことを心配する

☐ **above** 熟 above all 何よりも

☐ **absence** 名 欠席，欠如，不在

☐ **accept** 動 ①受け入れる ②同意する，認める

☐ **accident** 名 ①(不慮の)事故，災難 ②偶然

☐ **accustomed** 形 慣れた，いつもの be accustomed to ～に慣れている

☐ **Achmet** 名 アクメット《人名》

☐ **across** 熟 go across 横断する，渡る run across 走って渡る walk across ～を歩いて渡る

☐ **act** 動 ①行動する ②機能する ③演じる act for ～のために活動する，～の代理をする

☐ **active** 形 ①活動的な ②積極的な ③活動[作動]中の

☐ **ad** 略 advertisement (広告，宣伝)の略

☐ **add** 動 ①加える，足す ②足し算をする ③言い添える

☐ **address** 名 ①住所，アドレス ②演説

☐ **advance** 名 進歩，前進 in advance 前もって，あらかじめ

☐ **advantage** 名 有利な点[立場]，強み，優越

☐ **adventure** 名 冒険

☐ **advice** 名 忠告，助言，意見

☐ **affection** 名 愛情，感情

☐ **after** 熟 look after ～の世話をする，～に気をつける

☐ **afterwards** 副 その後，のちに

☐ **against** 熟 case against ～に対する訴訟

- **agate** 名メノウ
- **Agra** 名アグラ《インドの都市の名前》
- **Agra Fort** アーグラ城塞
- **agreement** 名①合意, 協定 ②一致
- **ah** 間《驚き・悲しみ・賞賛などを表して》ああ, やっぱり
- **aid** 動援助する, 助ける, 手伝う
- **Akbar, Dost** ドスト・アクバル《人名》
- **alive** 熟take ～ alive（人・動物などを）生け捕りにする
- **all** 熟above all 何よりも all day 一日中, 明けても暮れても all over 全て終わって, もうだめで all right 大丈夫で, よろしい, 申し分ない, わかった, 承知した all the time ずっと, いつも, その間ずっと All's well that ends well. 終わりよければ全てよし。《ことわざ》and all ～など, すっかり not at all 少しも～でない sit up all night 徹夜する take all the credit 手柄を独り占めする with all ～がありながら with all the will in the world 世界中のどんな意志を持ってしても
- **allow** 動①許す,《－ … to ～》…が～するのを可能にする, …に～させておく ②与える
- **along** 熟run along おいとまする, 立ち去る
- **aloud** 副大声で, (聞こえるように)声を出して
- **altogether** 副まったく, 全然, 全部で
- **amazing** 形驚くべき, 見事な
- **America** 名アメリカ《国名・大陸》
- **amount** 名①量, 額 ②《the －》合計
- **amuse** 動楽しませる
- **and all** ～など, すっかり
- **and so** そこで, それだから, それで
- **and so on** ～など, その他もろもろ
- **and yet** それなのに, それにもかかわらず
- **Andaman Islands** アンダマン諸島
- **Andaman prison** アンダマン刑務所
- **Andamans** 名アンダマン諸島
- **anger** 名怒り
- **angrily** 副怒って, 腹立たしげに
- **angry** 熟get angry 腹を立てる
- **anxious** 形①心配な, 不安な ②切望して
- **any** 熟if any もしあれば, あったとしても
- **anyone** 代①《疑問文・条件節で》誰か ②《否定文で》誰も（～ない）③《肯定文で》誰でも
- **anything but** ～のほかは何でも, 少しも～でない
- **anything else** ほかの何か
- **anyway** 副①いずれにせよ, ともかく ②どんな方法でも
- **anywhere** 副どこかへ[に], どこにも, どこへも, どこにでも
- **appear** 動①現れる, 見えてくる ②(～のように)見える, ～らしい
- **appearance** 名①現れること, 出現 ②外見, 印象
- **argue** 動①論じる, 議論する ②主張する
- **army** 名軍隊,《the －》陸軍
- **around** 熟carry around 持ち歩く go around 動き回る, あちらこちらに行く, 回り道をする, (障害)を回避する turn around 振り向く, 向きを変える, 方向転換する walk around 歩き回る, ぶらぶら歩く
- **arrest** 動逮捕する 名逮捕 under arrest 逮捕されて
- **arrive in** ～に着く

□ **article** 名①（法令・誓約などの）箇条, 項目 ②（新聞・雑誌などの）記事, 論文

□ **as** 熟 as ～ as ever 相変わらず, これまでのように as ～ as one can できる限り～ as bitter as a man could be 人一倍苦々しく as far as ～と同じくらい遠く, ～まで, ～する限り（では）as for ～に関しては, ～はどうかと言うと as if あたかも～のように, まるで～みたいに as much as ～と同じだけ as though あたかも～のように, まるで～みたいに as to ～に関しては, ～については, ～に応じて as usual いつものように, 相変わらず as well なお, その上, 同様に as well as ～と同様に just as（ちょうど）～のとおり see ～ as ... ～を…と考える such as ～ たとえば～, ～のような such ～ as ... …のような～

□ **ash** 名①灰, 燃えかす ②《-es》遺骨, なきがら

□ **ashore** 副岸に, 陸上に

□ **aside** 副わきへ（に）, 離れて

□ **assist** 動手伝う, 列席する, 援助する

□ **associate** 名仲間, 組合員

□ **astonishment** 名驚き

□ **at** 熟 at ease 心配なく at last ついに, とうとう at least 少なくとも at once すぐに, 同時に at one time ある時には, かつては at peace 平和に, 安らかに, 心穏やかで at that moment その時に, その瞬間に at that time その時 at the last moment 最後の瞬間に, 土壇場で at this point 現在のところ at times 時には

□ **Athelney Jones** アセルニー・ジョーンズ《人名》

□ **attack** 動①襲う, 攻める ②非難する ③（病気が）おかす

□ **attention** 名①注意, 集中 ②配慮, 手当て, 世話

□ **Aurora** 名オーロラ号《蒸気船の名》

□ **available** 形利用［使用・入手］できる, 得られる

□ **await** 動待つ, 待ち受ける

□ **aware** 形①気がついて, 知って ②（～の）認識のある

□ **away** 熟 be worn away 摩耗する come away ～から離れて行く get away 逃げる, 逃亡する, 離れる go away 立ち去る put away 片づける, 取っておく run away 走り去る, 逃げ出す

B

□ **back** 熟 back end 後端, 後部 back file バックナンバーのファイル bring back 戻す, 呼び戻す, 持ち帰る come back 戻る come back to ～へ帰ってくる, ～に戻る get back 戻る, 帰る go back on（人を）裏切る go back to ～に帰る［戻る］, ～に遡る（中断していた作業に）再び取り掛かる hold back（事実・本心などを）隠す［秘密にする・しまっておく］, 本当のことを言わない lean back 後ろにもたれる take back ①取り戻す ②（言葉, 約束を）取り消す, 撤回する

□ **backward** 副後方へ, 逆に, 後ろ向きに

□ **backwards** 副後方へ, 逆に, 後ろ向きに

□ **bad luck** 災難, 不運, 悪運

□ **badly** 副①悪く, まずく, へたに ②とても, ひどく

□ **Baker Street** ベーカー街《ロンドンの地名, ホームズとワトソンの住む家がある》

□ **Baker Street irregulars** ベーカー街非正規隊

□ **bald** 形①はげた ②すり減った, （木に）葉がない

□ **bald-headed** 形頭のはげた

112

☐ **bargain** 名 ①バーゲン, 安売り ②駆け引き

☐ **bark** 名 ①ほえる声, どなり声 ②木の皮 動ほえる, どなる

☐ **barrel** 名 ①たる, 1たるの分量 ②バレル《容量の単位》

☐ **Bartholomew Sholto** パーソロミュー・ショルトー《人名》

☐ **beard** 名あごひげ

☐ **beast** 名 ①動物, けもの ②けもののような人, 非常にいやな人[物]

☐ **beat** 動 ①打つ, 鼓動する ②打ち負かす

☐ **beauty** 名 ①美, 美しい人[物] ②《the –》美点

☐ **because of** ～のために, ～の理由で

☐ **bed** 熟 go to bed 床につく, 寝る

☐ **bedside** 名寝台のそば, まくら元

☐ **beginning** 名初め, 始まり

☐ **behalf** 名利益 on behalf of ～のために, ～に代わって

☐ **behind** 前 ①～の後ろに, ～の背後に ②～に遅れて, ～に劣って 副①後ろに, 背後に ②遅れて, 劣って

☐ **being** 動 be (～である) の現在分詞 名存在, 生命, 人間

☐ **belong** 動《– to ～》～に属する, ～のものである

☐ **below** 副下に[へ]

☐ **Benares metal-work** バラナシの金属細工

☐ **bend** 動 ①曲がる, 曲げる ②屈服する[させる] bend over かがむ, 腰をかがめる, ～に身をかがめる

☐ **beneath** 副下に, 劣って

☐ **bent** 形曲がった

☐ **Bernstone, Mrs.** バーンストン夫人《人名》

☐ **beside** 前 ①～のそばに, ～と並んで ②～と比べると ③～とはずれて

☐ **besides** 副 ①～に加えて, ～のほかに ②《否定文・疑問文で》～を除いて

☐ **best** 熟 do one's best 全力を尽くす

☐ **best-preserved** 形保存状態の極めて良い

☐ **better** 熟 get better (病気などが) 良くなる had better ～したほうが身のためだ, ～しなさい

☐ **between A and B** AとBの間に

☐ **beyond** 副向こうに

☐ **bit** bite (かむ) の過去, 過去分詞

☐ **bitter** 形 ①にがい ②つらい as bitter as a man could be 人一倍苦々しく

☐ **black or blue** 人種や肌の色に関係なく《blue=「青人」はインド人やアジア人を指す軽蔑語》

☐ **Blair Island** ブレア島

☐ **blame** 動とがめる, 非難する

☐ **blessing** 名 ①(神の) 恵み, 加護 ②祝福の祈り ③(食前・食後の) 祈り

☐ **blind** 動 ①目をくらます ②わからなくさせる

☐ **blink** 動目をパチパチさせる

☐ **blonde** 形 (女性が) 金髪の, ブロンドの, (皮膚が) 色白の

☐ **blood** 名 ①血, 血液 ②血統, 家柄 ③気質

☐ **blood-relation** 名血族の者

☐ **blow** 名 ①(風の) ひと吹き, 突風 ②(楽器の) 吹奏 ③打撃

☐ **blowpipe** 名吹き筒

☐ **blow-pipe** 名吹き筒

☐ **blue** 熟 black or blue 人種や肌の色に関係なく《blue=「青人」はインド人やアジア人を指す軽蔑語》

☐ **board** 名 ①板, 掲示板 ②委員会, 重役会 on board (乗り物などに) 乗って, 搭乗して

☐ **boarding house** 宿, 下宿屋

A
B
C
D
E
F
G
H
I
J
K
L
M
N
O
P
Q
R
S
T
U
V
W
X
Y
Z

113

- □ **boat-length** 名 艇身
- □ **boatman** 名 (貸し)ボート屋, ボートの漕ぎ手, 船頭
- □ **bodyguard** 名 ボディーガード, 護衛
- □ **boss** 名 上司, 親方, 監督
- □ **both A and B** AもBも
- □ **both of them** 彼ら[それら]両方とも
- □ **bother** 動 悩ます, 困惑させる
- □ **bottom** 名 ①底, 下部, すそ野, ふもと, 最下位, 根底 ②尻
- □ **brave** 形 勇敢な
- □ **break open** (金庫などを)こじ開ける
- □ **breath** 名 ①息, 呼吸 ②《a-》(風の)そよぎ, 気配, きざし
- □ **breathing** 名 ①呼吸, 息づかい ②《a-》ひと息の間, ちょっとの間
- □ **breed** 名 品種, 血統 **mixed breed** 混血, 雑種
- □ **brick** 名 レンガ, レンガ状のもの
- □ **briefly** 副 短く, 簡潔に
- □ **bring back** 戻す, 呼び戻す, 持ち帰る
- □ **British** 名 英国人
- □ **building** 名 建物, 建造物, ビルディング
- □ **bullet** 名 銃弾, 弾丸状のもの
- □ **bully** 動 いじめる, おどす
- □ **bump** 動 (～に)ぶつかる、(～を)ドンとぶつける
- □ **bundle** 名 束, 包み, 一巻き
- □ **buried** 形 埋められた
- □ **burning** 動 burn(燃える)の現在分詞 形 ①燃えている, 燃えるように暑い ②のどが渇いた, 激しい
- □ **burst** 動 ①爆発する[させる] ②破裂する[させる] **burst into** ～に飛び込む, 急に～する
- □ **but** 熟 **anything but** ～のほかは何でも, 少しも～でない **not ~ but ...** ～ではなくて…
- □ **by** 熟 **by oneself** 一人で, 自分だけで, 独力で **by the time** ～する時までに **by the way** ところで, ついでに, 途中で **by then** その時までに **by this time** この時までに, もうすでに **drop by** 立ち寄る **followed by** その後に～が続いて **stand by** そばに立つ, 傍観する, 待機する **stop by** 途中で立ち寄る, ちょっと訪ねる

C

- □ **cab** 名 タクシー
- □ **cabin** 名 (丸太作りの)小屋, 船室, キャビン
- □ **Calcutta** 名 カルカッタ《地名。現在のコルカタ》
- □ **call for** ～を求める, 訴える, ～を呼び求める, 呼び出す
- □ **call in** ～を呼ぶ, ～に立ち寄る
- □ **calm** 形 穏やかな, 落ち着いた 動 静まる, 静める
- □ **calmly** 副 落ち着いて, 静かに
- □ **can** 熟 **as ~ as one can** できる限り, ～する **can do nothing** どうしようもない **Can I ~?** ～してもよいですか。
- □ **canoe** 名 カヌー
- □ **captain** 名 長, 船長, 首領, 主将
- □ **Captain Morstan** モースタン大尉
- □ **careless** 形 不注意な, うかつな
- □ **carry around** 持ち歩く
- □ **carry into** ～の中に運び入れる
- □ **carry out** 外へ運び出す, [計画を]実行する
- □ **case** 熟 **case against** ～に対する訴訟 **in case of** ～の場合には、～に備えて **the case is closed** 一件落着
- □ **catch hold of** ～をつかむ, 捕らえる

□ **ceiling** 名①天井 ②上限, 最高価格

□ **certain** 形①確実な, 必ず〜する ②(人が)確信した ③ある ④いくらかの

□ **certainly** 副①確かに, 必ず ②《返答に用いて》もちろん, そのとおり, 承知しました

□ **challenge** 動挑む, 試す

□ **chapter** 名(書物の)章

□ **character** 名①特性, 個性 ②(小説・劇などの)登場人物 ③文字, 記号 ④品性, 人格

□ **charge** 名①請求金額, 料金 ②責任 ③非難, 告発 **clear someone of a charge** (人)に対する告訴を取り下げる

□ **charm** 動魅了する

□ **charming** 形魅力的な, チャーミングな

□ **chase** 動①追跡する, 追い[探し]求める ②追い立てる

□ **check** 動①照合する, 検査する ②阻止[妨害]する ③(所持品を)預ける **check into** (ホテルなどに)チェックインする **check on** 〜を調べる

□ **chemical** 形化学の, 化学的な

□ **chest** 名①大きな箱, 戸棚, たんす ②金庫 ③胸, 肺

□ **chin** 名あご

□ **choice** 名選択(の範囲・自由), えり好み, 選ばれた人[物]

□ **church-going** 形教会通いの

□ **cigar** 名葉巻

□ **cigarette** 名(紙巻)たばこ

□ **circle** 名①円, 円周, 輪 ②循環, 軌道 ③仲間, サークル

□ **civilian** 名一般市民, 民間人

□ **clear** 形①はっきりした, 明白な ②澄んだ ③(よく)晴れた 動①はっきりさせる ②片づける ③晴れる **clear someone of a charge** (人)に対する告訴を取り下げる 副①はっ

きりと ②すっかり, 完全に

□ **clearly** 副①明らかに, はっきりと ②《返答に用いて》そのとおり

□ **clever** 形①頭のよい, 利口な ②器用な, 上手な

□ **climbing** 動climb(登る)の現在分詞 名登ること, 登山

□ **closed** 動close(閉まる)の過去, 過去分詞 形閉じた, 閉鎖した **the case is closed** 一件落着

□ **closely** 副①密接に ②念入りに, 詳しく ③ぴったりと

□ **closer and closer** どんどん近づく

□ **clue** 名手がかり, 糸口

□ **coast** 名海岸, 沿岸 **off the coast** 〜沖に[で]

□ **cocaine** 名コカイン

□ **collection** 名収集, 収蔵物

□ **column** 名①コラム ②(新聞などの)縦の段[行・列] ③(円)柱

□ **come** 熟 come about 起こる come and 〜しに行く come away 〜から離れて行く come back 戻る come back to 〜へ帰ってくる, 〜に戻る come down 下りて来る come for 〜の目的で来る, 〜を取りに来る come forward 申し出る, 届け出る come in 中にはいる, やってくる, 出回る come into 〜にはいってくる come on ①いいかげんにしろ, もうよせ, さあ来なさい ②(人)に偶然出合う come out 出てくる, 出掛ける, 姿を現す, 発行される come up 近づいてくる, 階上に行く, 浮上する, 水面へ上ってくる come upon (人)に偶然出合う **It's come to this.** この始末だ。／こんなことになってしまった。

□ **coming** 動come(来る)の現在分詞 名到来, 来ること

□ **command** 名命令, 指揮(権) **in command of** 〜を指揮している

□ **commander** 名司令官, 指揮官

THE SIGN OF THE FOUR

□ **common sense** 常識

□ **companion** 图 友, 仲間, 連れ ②添えもの, つきもの

□ **completely** 副 完全に, すっかり

□ **concern** 動 ①関係する, 《be -ed in [with] 〜》〜に関係している ②心配させる, 《be -ed about [for] 〜》〜を心配する 图 ①関心事 ②関心, 心配 ③関係, 重要性

□ **condition** 图 ①(健康) 状態, 境遇 ②〈-s〉状況, 様子 ③条件

□ **confess** 動 (隠し事などを) 告白する, 打ち明ける, 白状する

□ **confession** 图 告白, 自白

□ **confidence** 图 自信, 確信, 信頼, 信用度

□ **confident** 形 自信のある, 自信に満ちた

□ **confidently** 副 確信して, 自信をもって, 大胆に

□ **confirm** 動 確かめる, 確かにする

□ **confirmed** 形 〔真実性などが〕確認 [立証] された

□ **confused** 形 困惑した, 混乱した

□ **congratulate** 動 祝う, 祝辞を述べる

□ **congratulation** 图 祝賀, 祝い, 《-s》祝いの言葉

□ **connected** 動 connect (つながる) の過去, 過去分詞 形 結合した, 関係のある

□ **construction** 图 構造, 建設, 工事, 建物

□ **consulting** 形 ①相談の ②診察の ③顧問の **consulting detective** 探偵

□ **contain** 動 ①含む, 入っている ②(感情などを) 抑える

□ **container** 图 ①容器, 入れ物 ②(輸送用) コンテナ

□ **control** 图 ①管理, 支配 (力) ②抑制

□ **conversation** 图 会話, 会談

□ **coolly** 副 冷静に, 冷たく

□ **could** 熟 **as bitter as a man could be** 人一倍苦々しく **could have done** 〜だったかもしれない 《仮定法》 **Could you 〜?** 〜してくださいますか。 **How could 〜?** 何だって〜なんてことがありえようか? **If +《主語》+ could** 〜できればなあ《仮定法》

□ **couple** 图 ①2つ, 対 ②夫婦, 一組 ③数個 **a couple of** 2, 3の

□ **course** 熟 **of course** もちろん, 当然

□ **court** 图 ①中庭, コート ②法廷, 裁判所 ③宮廷, 宮殿

□ **cover** 動 ①覆う, 包む, 隠す ②扱う, (〜に) わたる, 及ぶ ③代わりを務める ④補う

□ **cover-up** 图 隠蔽, もみ消し

□ **cracked** 形 砕けた, ひび割れた

□ **crazy** 形 ①狂気の, ばかげた, 無茶な ②夢中の, 熱狂的な

□ **credit** 图 ①信用, 評判, 名声 ②掛け売り, 信用貸し **take all the credit** 手柄を独り占めする

□ **creosote** 图 クレオソート《防腐薬, 鎮痛薬などに用いられる化学物質》

□ **crime** 图 ①(法律上の) 罪, 犯罪 ②悪事, よくない行為

□ **criminal** 图 犯罪者, 犯人

□ **crocodile** 图 クロコダイル

□ **crown** 图 ①冠 ②《the – 》王位 ③頂, 頂上

□ **cruel** 形 残酷な, 厳しい

□ **cry out** 叫ぶ

□ **crying** 图 泣き叫び, 号泣

□ **cupboard** 图 食器棚, 戸棚

□ **curious** 形 好奇心の強い, 珍しい, 奇妙な, 知りたがる

□ **curse** 動 のろう, ののしる

□ **cut off** 切断する, 切り離す

116

WORD LIST

D

- □ **dart** 名投げ矢, 投げ槍,《-s》ダーツ
- □ **day** 熟 **all day** 一日中, 明けても暮れても **day and night** 昼も夜も **one day**（過去の）ある日,（未来の）いつか
- □ **dead** 熟 **fall dead** 倒れて死ぬ
- □ **death** 名①死, 死ぬこと ②《the-》終えん, 消滅 **to death** 死ぬまで, 死ぬほど
- □ **decide to do** ～することに決める
- □ **deck** 名（船の）デッキ, 甲板, 階, 床
- □ **decoration** 名装飾, 飾りつけ
- □ **deduction** 名①差し引き（額）②推論
- □ **defeat** 動①打ち破る, 負かす ②だめにする
- □ **delay** 名遅延, 延期, 猶予
- □ **delighted** 形喜んでいる, うれしそうな
- □ **demand** 動①要求する, 尋ねる ②必要とする
- □ **demonstration** 名①論証, 証明 ②デモンストレーション, 実演 ③デモ, 示威運動
- □ **deny** 動否定する, 断る, 受けつけない
- □ **depressed** 形がっかりした, 落胆した
- □ **describe** 動（言葉で）描写する, 特色を述べる, 説明する
- □ **description** 名（言葉で）記述（すること）, 描写（すること）
- □ **deserted** 形人影のない, さびれた
- □ **destine** 動①運命づける ②《be-d to》～する運命である
- □ **destroy** 動破壊する, 絶滅させる, 無効にする
- □ **detail** 名①細部,《-s》詳細 ②《-s》個人情報 **to the last detail** 細かい点の一つ一つに至るまで

- □ **detective** 名探偵, 刑事 **consulting detective** 探偵 形探偵の
- □ **determination** 名決心, 決定
- □ **devilish** 形①悪魔のような ②のろわしい, 極悪な
- □ **diamond** 名①ダイヤモンド ②ひし形
- □ **die of** ～がもとで死ぬ
- □ **difficulty** 名①むずかしさ ②難局, 支障, 苦情, 異議 ③《-ties》財政困難
- □ **dip** 動①ちょっと浸す, さっとつける ②（値段などが）下がる
- □ **direction** 名①方向, 方角 ②《-s》指示, 説明書 ③指導, 指揮
- □ **dirt** 名①汚れ, 泥, ごみ ②土 ③悪口, 中傷
- □ **dirty** 形①汚い, 汚れた ②卑劣な, 不正な
- □ **disappear** 動見えなくなる, 姿を消す, なくなる
- □ **disappearance** 名見えなくなること, 消失, 失踪
- □ **disappointed** 形がっかりした, 失望した
- □ **discoverer** 名発見者
- □ **discovery** 名発見
- □ **disguise** 動変装させる, 隠す 名変装（すること）, 見せかけ
- □ **disloyal** 形不実な
- □ **distrustful** 形不信の念を抱いている
- □ **divide** 動分かれる, 分ける, 割れる, 割る
- □ **division** 名①分割 ②部門 ③境界 ④割り算
- □ **door** 熟 **knock on the door** ドアをノックする
- □ **doorbell** 名玄関の呼び鈴[ベル]
- □ **doorman** 名（ホテルの）ドアマン
- □ **doorway** 名戸口, 玄関, 出入り口

117

□ **Dost Akbar** ドスト・アクバル《人名》

□ **doubt** 图 ①疑い, 不確かなこと ②未解決点, 困難

□ **down** 熟 **come down** 下りて来る **down on one's luck** つきに見放されて **go down** 下に降りる **hang down** ぶら下がる **lay down** ①下に置く, 横たえる ②裏切る **let down** 期待を裏切る, 失望させる **lie down** 横たわる, 横になる **look down upon** 見下ろす, 俯瞰する **put down** 下に置く, 下ろす **track down** 見つけ出す, 追い詰める **turn down** (音量などを) 小さくする, 弱くする, 拒絶する **up and down** 上がったり下がったり, 行ったり来たり, あちこちと **walk up and down** 行ったり来たりする **write down** 書き留める

□ **downstairs** 剾 階下で, 下の部屋で

□ **Dr.** 略 ～博士, 《医者に対して》～先生

□ **drag** 動 ①引きずる ②のろのろ動く [動かす]

□ **drama** 图 劇, 演劇, ドラマ, 劇的な事件

□ **draw up** (車を) 止める

□ **drawn** 動 draw (引く) の過去分詞

□ **dream of** ～を夢見る

□ **dreamland** 图 夢の国, 眠り

□ **drew** 動 draw (引く) の過去

□ **dried** 動 dry (乾燥する) の過去, 過去分詞

□ **drive up** 車でやって来る

□ **driven** 動 drive (車で行く) の過去分詞

□ **drop by** 立ち寄る

□ **drop someone off at home** (人) を車で家まで送る

□ **drove** 動 drive (車で行く) の過去

□ **drug** 图 薬, 麻薬, 麻酔薬

□ **dryly** 剾 無味乾燥に, 冷淡に

□ **duck** 图 カモ, アヒル

□ **dusty** 形 ほこりだらけの

□ **duty** 图 ①義務 (感), 責任 ②職務, 任務, 関税 **off duty** 非番 [勤務時間外] に [で]

□ **dying** 形 死にかかっている, 消えそうな

E

□ **each** 熟 **each other** お互いに **on each side** それぞれの側に

□ **earn** 動 ①儲ける, 稼ぐ ② (名声を) 博す

□ **ease** 图 安心, 気楽 **at ease** 安心して, 心配なく

□ **easily** 剾 ①容易に, たやすく, 苦もなく ②気楽に

□ **edge** 图 ①刃 ②端, 縁

□ **eh** 圊 《略式》えっ (何ですか), もう一度言ってください《驚き・疑いを表したり, 相手に繰り返しを求める》

□ **either A or B** A かそれとも B

□ **elder** 形 年上の, 年長の

□ **eldest** 形 最年長の

□ **else** 熟 **anything else** ほかの何か **no one else** 他の誰一人として～しない

□ **emerald** 图 エメラルド

□ **emotional** 形 ①感情の, 心理的な ②感情的な, 感激しやすい

□ **employer** 图 雇主, 使用 [利用] する人

□ **empty ring** 心のこもっていないお祝い

□ **end** 熟 **All's well that ends well.** 終わりよければ全てよし。《ことわざ》 **back end** 後端, 後部

□ **endure** 動 ①我慢する, 耐え忍ぶ ②持ちこたえる

□ **enemy** 图 敵

□ **England** 图 ①イングランド ②英国

□ **Englishman** 图 イングランド人, イギリス人

□ **enough to do** 〜するのに十分な

□ **entirely** 副 完全に, まったく

□ **entry** 图 入ること, 入り口

□ **envelope** 图 封筒, 包み

□ **episode** 图 ①挿話, 出来事 ②(テレビ番組の)1回放映分 ③(シリーズ物の)第一話

□ **equally** 副 等しく, 平等に

□ **escape** 動 逃げる, 免れる, もれる 图 逃亡, 脱出, もれ

□ **European** 图 ヨーロッパ人

□ **even though** 〜であるけれども, 〜にもかかわらず

□ **ever** 熟 as 〜 as ever 相変わらず, これまでのように

□ **every time** 〜するときはいつも

□ **everyone** 代 誰でも, 皆

□ **everything** 代 すべてのこと[もの], 何でも, 何もかも

□ **evil** 形 ①邪悪な ②有害な, 不吉な

□ **exact** 形 正確な, 厳密な, きちょうめんな

□ **examine** 動 試験する, 調査[検査]する, 診察する

□ **example** 熟 for example たとえば

□ **except** 前 〜を除いて, 〜のほかは except for 〜を除いて, 〜がなければ 接 〜ということを除いて

□ **excited** 動 excite (興奮する)の過去, 過去分詞 形 興奮した, わくわくした

□ **excitement** 图 興奮(すること)

□ **exclaim** 動 ①(喜び・驚きなどで)声をあげる ②声高に激しく言う

□ **expect** 動 予期[予測]する, (当然のこととして)期待する

□ **expression** 图 ①表現, 表示, 表情 ②言い回し, 語句

□ **extra** 形 余分の, 臨時の

□ **extremely** 副 非常に, 極度に

□ **eye** 熟 keep an eye on 〜から目を離さない

□ **eyebrow** 图 まゆ(眉)

F

□ **faint** 動 気絶する

□ **fair** 形 ①正しい, 公平[正当]な ②快晴の ③色白の, 金髪の ④かなりの ⑤《古》美しい

□ **fall dead** 倒れて死ぬ

□ **fall over** 〜につまずく, 〜の上に倒れかかる

□ **fallen** 動 fall (落ちる)の過去分詞

□ **far** 熟 as far as 〜と同じくらい遠く, 〜まで, 〜する限り(では) far from 〜から遠い, 〜どころか far off ずっと遠くに, はるかかなたに how far どのくらいの距離か

□ **farmer** 图 農民, 農場経営者

□ **fat** 形 ①太った ②脂っこい ③分厚い

□ **fear** 图 ①恐れ ②心配, 不安 with fear 怖がって 動 ①恐れる ②心配する

□ **feature** 图 ①特徴, 特色 ②顔の一部, 《-s》顔立ち ③(ラジオ・テレビ・新聞などの)特集

□ **feeling** 動 feel (感じる)の現在分詞 图 ①感じ, 気持ち ②触感, 知覚 ③同情, 思いやり, 感受性

□ **feet** 熟 get to one's feet 立ち上がる jump to one's feet 飛び起きる

□ **fellow** 图 ①仲間, 同僚 ②人, やつ

□ **fever** 图 ①熱, 熱狂 ②熱病

□ **fierce-looking** 形 猛猛しい

□ **figure** 图 ①人[物]の姿, 形 ②図

(形) ③数字

□ **file** 名ファイル, 書類綴じ, 縦列
back file バックナンバーのファイル

□ **final** 形最後の, 決定的な

□ **find out** 見つけ出す, 気がつく, 知る, 調べる, 解明する

□ **firm** 形堅い, しっかりした, 断固とした **in a firm way** きっぱりと

□ **fist** 名こぶし, げんこつ

□ **fit** 動合致［適合］する, 合致させる

□ **fixed** 形①固定した, ゆるぎない
②八百長の

□ **flame** 名炎, (炎のような) 輝き

□ **flash** 名閃光, きらめき 動①閃光を発する ②さっと動く, ひらめく

□ **float** 動①浮く, 浮かぶ ②漂流する ③(心に) 浮かぶ ④《be ～ing》(うわさなどが) 広まる

□ **flow** 動流れ出る, 流れる, あふれる

□ **foggy** 形霧の多い, 霧の立ちこめた

□ **folk** 名①(生活様式を共にする) 人々 ②《one's -s》家族, 親類

□ **follow up** (人) の跡を追う

□ **followed by** その後に～が続いて

□ **following** 動follow (ついていく) の現在分詞 形《the –》次の, 次に続く

□ **fool** 名①ばか者, おろかな人 ②道化師 動ばかにする, だます, ふざける

□ **foothold** 名足がかり, 足場

□ **footmark** 名足跡

□ **footprint** 名足型, 足跡

□ **footstep** 名足音, 歩み

□ **for** 熟act for ～のために活動する, ～の代理をする as for ～に関しては, ～はどうかと言うと be ready for 準備が整って, ～に期待する call for ～を求める, 訴える, ～を呼び求める, 呼び出す come for ～の目的で来る, ～を取りに来る except for ～を除

いて, ～がなければ **for a while** しばらくの間, 少しの間 **for example** たとえば **for long** 長い間 **for nothing** ただで, 無料で, むだに **for oneself** 独力で, 自分のために **for some time** しばらくの間 **for that matter** ついでに言えば **for years** 何年も **for ～ years** ～年間, ～年にわたって **head for** ～に向かう, ～の方に進む **It is ～ for someone to ...** (人) が…するのは～だ **look for** ～を探す **lucky for** (人) にとってラッキーだったことには **on the lookout for** ～に目を光らせて **reason for** ～の理由 **see for yourself** 自分で確かめる **thank ～ for** ～に対して礼を言う **wait for** ～を待つ **what ... for** どんな目的で **wish for** 所望する

□ **force** 名力, 勢い 動①強制する, 力ずくで～する, 余儀なく～させる ②押しやる, 押し込む

□ **form** 動形づくる

□ **Forrester, Mrs.** 名フォレスター夫人

□ **fort** 名砦, 要塞

□ **fortune** 名①富, 財産 ②幸運, 繁栄, チャンス ③運命, 運勢

□ **forward** 副①前方に ②将来に向けて ③先へ, 進んで **come forward** 申し出る, 届け出る

□ **foster** 形里親の

□ **frankly** 副率直に, ありのままに

□ **free** 熟set free (人) を解放する, 釈放される, 自由の身になる

□ **freedom** 名①自由 ②束縛がないこと

□ **friend** 熟make friends with ～と友達になる

□ **friendship** 名友人であること, 友情

□ **frighten** 動驚かせる, びっくりさせる

□ **frightened** 形おびえた, びっくりした

□ **frightening** 形恐ろしい, どきっとさせる

□ **from** 熟 far from ～から遠い, ～どころか from time to time ときどき from ～ to ... ～から…まで hear from ～から手紙[電話・返事]をもらう keep someone from ～から(人)を阻む look from one to the other of us 私たちの顔を代わる代わる見る

□ **front** 熟 get in front of ～の正面に出る in front of ～の前に, ～の正面に

□ **fuel** 名①燃料 ②激情をあおるもの

□ **full of** 《be –》～で一杯である

□ **furniture** 名家具, 備品, 調度

□ **further** 副いっそう遠く, その上に, もっと

G

□ **gain** 動①得る, 増す ②進歩する, 進む

□ **gang** 名①群れ, 一団 ②ギャング, 暴力団 ③(子ども, 若者の) 遊び仲間, 非行少年グループ

□ **Ganges** 名ガンジス川

□ **gatekeeper** 名門番, 守衛

□ **gateway** 名出入り口, 道

□ **gem** 名宝石, 宝玉, すばらしいもの

□ **get** 熟 get angry 腹を立てる get at 届く, 入手する get away 逃げる, 逃亡する, 離れる get back 戻る, 帰る get better (病気などが) 良くなる get in 中に入る, 乗り込む get in front of ～の正面に出る get into ～に入る, 入り込む, ～に巻き込まれる get light 明るくなる get lost 迷子になる, 道に迷う get mixed up かかわり合いになる, 巻き添えを食う get near 接近する get on (電車などに) 乗る get out ①外に出る, 出て行く, 逃げ出す ②取り出す, 抜き出す get revenge 復しゅうする get there そ

こに到着する, 目的を達成する, 成功する get to (事)を始める, ～に達する[到着する] get to one's feet 立ち上がる get up 起き上がる, 立ち上がる get worse 悪化する

□ **giant** 名①巨人, 大男 ②巨匠

□ **glad to do** 《be –》～してうれしい, 喜んで～する

□ **glorious** 形①栄誉に満ちた, 輝かしい ②荘厳な, すばらしい

□ **go** 熟 go across 横断する, 渡る go and ～しに行く go around 動き回る, あちらこちらに行く, 回り道をする, (障害)を回避する go away 立ち去る go back on (人を)裏切る go back to ～に帰る[戻る], ～に遡る, (中断していた作業)に再び取り掛かる go doing ～をしに行く go down 下に降りる go home 帰宅する go in 中に入る, 開始する go into ～に入る, (仕事)に就く go off 出かける, 去る, 出発する go on 続く, 続ける, 進み続ける, 起こる, 発生する go on to ～に移る, ～に取り掛かる go out 外出する, 外へ出る go over to ～の前に[へ]行く, ～に出向いて行く go through 通り抜ける, 一つずつ順番に検討する go to bed 床につく, 寝る go up ①～に上がる, 登る ②～に近づく, 出かける ③(建物などが) 建つ, 立つ go up to ～まで行く, 近づく go with ～と一緒に行く, ～と調和する, ～にとても似合う go wrong 失敗する, 道を踏みはずす, 調子が悪くなる [let ～ go ～を放つ[解放する]]

□ **god** 熟 My God. おや, まあ Thank God. ありがたい

□ **gold** 名金, 金貨, 金製品, 金色 形金の, 金製の, 金色の

□ **good** 熟 make good use of ～をうまく[有効に]使う

□ **good-night** 間さようなら!, お休みなさい

□ **got** 熟 have got 持っている

□ **gotten** 動 get (得る)の過去分詞

121

□ **government** 名政治, 政府, 支配

□ **governor-general** 名(植民地などの)総督

□ **grave** 名墓

□ **Great Mogul** ムガール皇帝《ダイヤモンドの名前》

□ **greed** 名どん欲, 欲張り

□ **groan** 動①うめく, うなる ②ぶうぶう言う

□ **ground** 熟on the ground 地面に

□ **grow -er and -er** 〜にますます〜する

□ **guard** 名①警戒, 見張り ②番人 動番をする, 監視する, 守る

□ **guarded** 形保護された

□ **guardman** 名ガードマン(見張り)

□ **guilt** 名罪, 有罪, 犯罪

□ **guilty** 形有罪の, やましい

□ **gun** 名銃, 大砲

H

□ **ha** 間ほう, まあ, おや《驚き・悲しみ・不満・喜び・笑い声などを表す》

□ **habit** 名習慣, 癖, 気質

□ **had better** 〜したほうが身のためだ, 〜しなさい

□ **hairy** 形毛むくじゃらの, 毛製の

□ **halfway** 形中間[中途]の, 不完全な

□ **hall** 名公会堂, ホール, 大広間, 玄関

□ **halting** 形言葉がつかえる, もたつく

□ **hand over** 手渡す, 引き渡す, 譲渡する

□ **handcuffed** 形手錠をかけられた

□ **handkerchief** 名ハンカチ

□ **handle** 動①手を触れる ②操縦する, 取り扱う

□ **handprint** 名手形

□ **hang** 動かかる, かける, つるす, ぶら下がる **hang down** ぶら下がる

□ **happen to** たまたま〜する, 偶然〜する

□ **happy to do** 《be −》〜してうれしい, 喜んで〜する

□ **hard to** 〜し難い

□ **hardest hit** 最も大きな[ひどい]打撃[痛手]を受ける

□ **hardly** 副①ほとんど〜でない, わずかに ②厳しく, かろうじて

□ **harm** 動傷つける, 損なう

□ **hate** 名憎しみ

□ **hatred** 名憎しみ, 毛嫌い

□ **have** 熟could have done 〜だったかもしれない《仮定法》have got 持っている have nothing to do with 〜と何の関係もない have to do with 〜と関係がある should have done 〜すべきだった(のにしなかった)《仮定法》will have done 〜してしまっているだろう《未来完了形》

□ **head for** 〜に向かう, 〜の方に進む

□ **hear from** 〜から手紙[電話・返事]をもらう

□ **hearing** 動hear (聞く)の現在分詞 名①聞くこと, 聴取, 聴力 ②聴聞会, ヒアリング

□ **heart and soul** 全身全霊をかけて

□ **heavily** 副①重く, 重そうに, ひどく ②多量に

□ **height** 名①高さ, 身長 ②《the −》絶頂, 真っ盛り ③高台, 丘

□ **hell** 名地獄, 地獄のようなところ[状態]

□ **help 〜 to ...** 〜が…するのを助ける

□ **help 〜 with ...** …を〜の面で手伝う

□ **helper** 名助手, 助けになるもの

□ **helpless** 形無力の, 自分ではどうすることもできない

□ **here** 熟 here and there あちこちで here is ～ こちらは～です。Look here. ほら。ねえ。

□ **hesitate** 動ためらう, ちゅうちょする

□ **hidden** 動 hide（隠れる）の過去分詞 形隠れた, 秘密の

□ **hide** 動隠れる, 隠す, 隠れて見えない, 秘密にする

□ **high-pitched** 形かん高い

□ **Hindu** 名ヒンドゥー人, インド人

□ **hire** 動雇う, 賃借りする

□ **hit** 熟 hardest hit 最も大きな［ひどい］打撃［痛手］を受ける

□ **hmm** 間ふむ, ううむ《熟考・疑問・ためらいなどを表す》

□ **hold** 熟 catch hold of ～をつかむ, 捕らえる hold back（事実・本心などを）隠す［秘密にする・しまっておく］, 本当のことを言わない hold on しっかりつかまる hold out ①差し出す,（腕を）伸ばす ②持ちこたえる, 粘る, 耐える hold up ①維持する, 支える ②～を持ち上げる ③（指を）立てる

□ **Holmes, Sherlock** シャーロック・ホームズ《人名》

□ **home** 熟 drop someone off at home（人）を車で家まで送る go home 帰宅する take someone home（人）を家まで送る

□ **honor** 名①名誉, 光栄, 信用 ②節操, 自尊心 honor of doing ～する光栄［栄誉］

□ **honorable** 形①尊敬すべき, 立派な ②名誉ある ③高貴な

□ **hook** 名止め金, 釣り針

□ **Hope Town** ホープ・タウン《地名》

□ **horrible** 形恐ろしい, ひどい

□ **horror** 名①恐怖, ぞっとすること ②嫌悪

□ **horse-drawn** 形馬が引く

□ **housekeeper** 名家政婦

□ **how** 熟 How about ～? ～はどうですか。～しませんか。How could ～? 何だって～なんてことがありえようか？ how far どのくらいの距離か how to ～する方法 no matter how どんなに～であろうとも

□ **however** 接けれども, だが

□ **Hudson, Mrs.** ハドソン夫人

□ **humor** 名①ユーモア ②（一時的な）機嫌

□ **hundreds of** 何百もの～

□ **hung** 動 hang（かかる）の過去, 過去分詞

□ **hunt** 動狩る, 狩りをする, 探し求める

□ **hurry** 熟 in a hurry 急いで, あわてて

□ **hut** 名簡易住居, あばら屋, 山小屋

I

□ **ideal** 形理想的な, 申し分のない

□ **if** 熟 as if あたかも～のように, まるで～みたいに if any もしあれば, あったとしても see if ～かどうかを確かめる If +《主語》+ could ～できればなあ《仮定法》wonder if ～ではないかと思う

□ **imagine** 動想像する, 心に思い描く

□ **immediately** 副すぐに, ～するやいなや

□ **in** 熟 in a firm way きっぱりと in a hurry 急いで, あわてて in advance 前もって, あらかじめ in an instant たちまち, ただちに in case of ～の場合には, ～に備えて in command of ～を指揮している in front of ～の前に, ～の正面に in luck 運がよくて in silence 黙って, 沈黙のうちに in the meantime それまでは, 当分は in the world 世界で in this way このようにして in trouble 面倒な状況で, 困って

☐ **including** 前 ～を含めて, 込みで

☐ **increase** 動 増加［増強］する, 増やす, 増える

☐ **indeed** 副 ①実際, 本当に ②《強意》まったく

☐ **India** 名 インド《国名》

☐ **Indian** 名 ①インド人 ②（アメリカ）インディアン 形 ①インド（人）の ②（アメリカ）インディアンの

☐ **indigo-planter** 名 藍農場主

☐ **inform** 動 ①告げる, 知らせる ②密告する

☐ **injured** 形 負傷した,（名誉・感情などを）損ねられた

☐ **ink** 名 インク

☐ **inner** 形 ①内部の ②心の中の

☐ **insect** 名 虫, 昆虫

☐ **instant** 名 瞬間, 寸時 in an instant たちまち, ただちに

☐ **instantly** 副 すぐに, 即座に

☐ **intake** 名 吸い込み

☐ **intention** 名 ①意図,（～する）つもり ②心構え

☐ **interested** 形 興味を持った, 関心のある be interested in ～に興味［関心］がある

☐ **interesting** 形 おもしろい, 興味を起こさせる

☐ **into** 熟 burst into ～に飛び込む, 急に～する carry into ～の中に運び入れる check into （ホテルなどに）チェックインする come into ～に入ってくる get into ～に入る, 入り込む, ～に巻き込まれる go into ～に入る,（仕事）に就く look into ①～を検討する, ～を研究する ②～の中を見る, ～をのぞき込む run into （思いがけず）～に出会う, ～に駆け込む, ～の中に走って入る

☐ **involved** 形 ①巻き込まれている, 関連する ②入り組んだ, 込み入っている

☐ **iron** 名 ①鉄, 鉄製のもの ②アイロン 形 鉄の, 鉄製の

☐ **irregular** 形 不規則な, ふぞろいの

☐ **islander** 名 島の住民

☐ **isolated** 形 隔離した, 孤立した

☐ **It is ～ for someone to ...** （人）が～するのは～だ

☐ **It's come to this.** この始末だ。／こんなことになってしまった。

J

☐ **Jacobson's Yard** ジョイコブソンズ造船所

☐ **jail** 名 刑務所

☐ **jewel** 名 宝石, 貴重な人［物］

☐ **jewelry** 名 宝石, 宝飾品類

☐ **Jiddah** 名 ジッダ《サウジアラビアの地名》

☐ **Jim** 名 ジム《人名》

☐ **John Sholto, Major** ジョン・ショルトー少佐

☐ **jokingly** 副 冗談に, しゃれて

☐ **Jonathan Small** ジョナサン・スモール《人名》

☐ **Jones, Athelney** アセルニー・ジョーンズ《人名》

☐ **journey** 名 ①（遠い目的地への）旅 ②行程

☐ **joyfully** 副 うれしそうに, 喜んで

☐ **judgment** 名 ①判断, 意見 ②裁判, 判決

☐ **jump to one's feet** 飛び起きる

☐ **just as** （ちょうど）であろうとおり

☐ **just then** そのとたんに

☐ **justice** 名 ①公平, 公正, 正当, 正義 ②司法, 裁判（官）

K

- ☐ **keep an eye on** 〜から目を離さない
- ☐ **keep someone from** 〜から（人）を阻む
- ☐ **keyhole** 图かぎ穴
- ☐ **Khan, Abdullah** アブドーラ・カーン《人名》
- ☐ **killer** 图殺人者［犯］
- ☐ **killing** 動killの（殺す）の現在分詞 图殺害, 殺人
- ☐ **kind of** ある程度, いくらか, 〜のようなもの［人］
- ☐ **kindly** 副親切に, 優しく
- ☐ **km** 图キロメートル《単位》
- ☐ **knee** 图ひざ
- ☐ **knife** 图ナイフ, 小刀, 包丁, 短剣
- ☐ **knock** 動ノックする, たたく, ぶつける **knock on the door** ドアをノックする 图打つこと, 戸をたたくこと［音］
- ☐ **know nothing of** 〜のことを知らない
- ☐ **know of** 〜について知っている
- ☐ **knowledge** 图知識, 理解, 学問

L

- ☐ **£** 略ポンド《イギリスの貨幣単位》
- ☐ **laboratory** 图実験室, 研究室
- ☐ **ladder** 图はしご, はしご状のもの
- ☐ **laid** 動lay（置く）の過去, 過去分詞
- ☐ **Lal Rao** ラル・ラオ《人名》
- ☐ **lamp** 图ランプ, 灯火
- ☐ **landing** 動land（上陸する）の現在分詞
- ☐ **landlady** 图女家主, 女主人
- ☐ **lantern** 图手提げランプ, ランタン
- ☐ **last** 熟 **at last** ついに, とうとう **at the last moment** 最後の瞬間に, 土壇場で **the last time** この前〜したとき **to the last detail** 細かい点の一つ一つに至るまで
- ☐ **laughter** 图笑い（声）
- ☐ **lay** 動①置く, 横たえる, 敷く ②整える ③卵を産む ④lie（横たわる）の過去 **lay down** ①下に置く, 横たえる ②裏切る
- ☐ **lead out** 外へ連れて行く
- ☐ **lead out onto** 〜の方へ導く
- ☐ **lead the way** 先に立って導く, 案内する, 率先する
- ☐ **lead to** 〜に至る, 〜に通じる, 〜を引き起こす
- ☐ **lean** 動①もたれる, 寄りかかる ②傾く, 傾ける **lean back** 後ろにもたれる
- ☐ **least** 图最小, 最少 **at least** 少なくとも
- ☐ **leave in** 〜をそのままにしておく
- ☐ **led** 動lead（導く）の過去, 過去分詞
- ☐ **left-hand** 形①左側の, 左方向の ②左手の, 左利きの
- ☐ **length** 图長さ, 縦, たけ, 距離
- ☐ **let down** 期待を裏切る, 失望させる
- ☐ **let loose** 解放する, 好きなようにさせる
- ☐ **let 〜 go** 〜を放す［解放する］
- ☐ **let us** どうか私たちに〜させてください
- ☐ **lid** 图（箱, なべなどの）ふた
- ☐ **lie** 動①うそをつく ②横たわる, 寝る ③（ある状態に）ある, 存在する **lie down** 横たわる, 横になる **lie off**（陸地などから）離れたところに位置する 图うそ, 詐欺 **tell a lie** うそをつく
- ☐ **lift** 動①持ち上げる, 上がる ②取り除く, 撤廃する
- ☐ **light** 熟 **get light** 明るくなる

125

- □ **lightly** 副 ①軽く, そっと ②軽率に

- □ **like** 熟 like this このような, こんなふうに look like ～のように見える, ～に似ている would like to ～したいと思う

- □ **liking** 名 好意, 好感

- □ **link** 名 ①(鎖の)輪 ②リンク ③相互[因果]関係 missing link 系列を完成するのに欠けているもの, 失われた環

- □ **lip** 名 唇, 《-s》口

- □ **list** 名 名簿, 目録, 一覧表

- □ **living** 形 ①生きている, 現存の ②使用されている ③そっくりの

- □ **lodge** 名 ①番小屋 ②山小屋

- □ **London** 名 ロンドン《英国の首都》

- □ **lonely** 形 ①孤独な, 心さびしい ②ひっそりした, 人里離れた

- □ **long** 熟 for long 長い間

- □ **longer** 熟 no longer もはや～でない[～しない]

- □ **long-haired** 形 長毛の

- □ **look** 熟 Look here. ほら。ねえ。look after ～の世話をする, ～に気をつける look down upon 見下ろす, 俯瞰する look for ～を探す look from one to the other of us 私たちの顔を代わる代わる見る look in 中を見る, 立ち寄る look into ①～を検討する, ～を研究する ②～の中を見る, ～をのぞき込む look like ～のように見える, ～に似ている look out ①外を見る ②気をつける, 注意する look out of (窓などから) 外を見る look over at ～の方を見る look through ～をのぞき込む look to ～しようとする look up 見上げる, 調べる look up to ～を仰ぎ見る look upon ～を見る, 見つめる

- □ **lookout** 名 ①見張り, 警戒 ②見込み on the lookout for ～に目を光らせて

- □ **loose** 形 自由な, ゆるんだ, あいま

いな 動 ほどく, 解き放つ let loose 解放する, 好きなようにさせる

- □ **loosely** 副 ①ゆるく, おおざっぱに ②だらしなく

- □ **loss** 名 ①損失(額・物), 損害, 浪費 ②失敗, 敗北

- □ **lost** 熟 get lost 迷子になる, 道に迷う

- □ **lot** 熟 a lot of たくさんの～ lots of たくさんの～

- □ **lower** 形 もっと低い, 下級の, 劣った 動 下げる, 低くする

- □ **luck** 熟 bad luck 災難, 不運, 悪運 down on one's luck つきに見放されて in luck 運がよくて out of luck 不運で, (運が)ついていない

- □ **luckily** 副 運よく, 幸いにも

- □ **lucky for** (人)にとってラッキーだったことには

- □ **lumber** 名 ①材木, 用材 ②がらくた lumber yard 材木置き場

- □ **Lyceum Theatre** ライシーアム劇場

- □ **lying** 動 lie (うそをつく・横たわる)の現在分詞

M

- □ **Madras** 名 マドラス《地名, 現在のチェンナイ》

- □ **Mahomet Singh** マホメット・シン《人名》

- □ **main** 形 主な, 主要な

- □ **major** 名 ①陸軍少佐 ②専攻科目

- □ **Major John Sholto** ジョン・ショルトー少佐

- □ **make** 熟 make a mistake 間違いをする make friends with ～と友達になる make good use of ～をうまく[有効に]使う make noise 音を立てる make one's way 進む, 行く, 成功する make out 作り上げる, 認

識する, 見分ける **make sure** 確かめる, 確認する **make up one's mind** 決心する **make way** 道を譲る[あける], 前進する

□ **man** 熟 **as bitter as a man could be** 人一倍苦々しく **wild man** 野蛮人

□ **many** 熟 **so many** 非常に多くの

□ **mark** 名 ①印, 記号, 跡 ②点数 ③特色

□ **marry** 動 結婚する

□ **Mary Morstan** メアリー・モースタン《人名》

□ **master** 名 主人, 雇い主, 師, 名匠

□ **match** 名 ①試合, 勝負 ②相手, 釣り合うもの ③マッチ(棒) 動 ①〜に匹敵する ②調和する, 釣り合う ③(〜を…と)勝負させる

□ **matter** 熟 **a matter of** 〜の問題 **for that matter** ついでに言えば **no matter how** どんなに〜であろうとも

□ **maximum** 名 最大(限), 最高

□ **May I ~?** 〜してもよいですか。

□ **meantime** 名 合間, その間 **in the meantime** それまでは, 当分は

□ **meeting** 名 ①集まり, ミーティング, 面会 ②競技会

□ **mention** 動 (〜について)述べる, 言及する

□ **merchant** 名 商人, 貿易商

□ **mere** 形 単なる, ほんの, まったく 〜にすぎない

□ **merry** 形 陽気な, 愉快な, 快活な

□ **metal** 名 金属, 合金

□ **metal-work** 名 金属細工(物)

□ **meter** 名 ①メートル《長さの単位》 ②計量器, 計量する人

□ **method** 名 ①方法, 手段 ②秩序, 体系

□ **middle** 形 中間の, 中央の

□ **middle-aged** 形 中高年の

□ **might** 動 《mayの過去》①〜かもしれない ②〜してもよい, 〜できる

□ **mile** 名 ①マイル《長さの単位。 1,609m》②(-s)かなりの距離

□ **mind** 名 ①心, 精神, 考え ②知性 **make up one's mind** 決心する

□ **misfortune** 名 不運, 不幸, 災難

□ **missing** 動 miss (失敗する)の現在分詞 形 欠けている, 行方不明の

□ **missing link** 系列を完成するのに欠けているもの, 失われた環

□ **mistake** 熟 **make a mistake** 間違いをする

□ **mix** 動 ①混ざる, 混ぜる ②(〜を)一緒にする

□ **mixed** 動 mix (混ざる)の過去, 過去分詞 形 混合の, 混ざった **get mixed up** かかわり合いになる, 巻き添えを食う **mixed breed** 混血, 雑種

□ **moat** 名 堀

□ **modern** 形 現代[近代]の, 現代的な, 最近の

□ **Mogul, Great** ムガール皇帝《ダイヤモンドの名前》

□ **mole** 名 ①モグラ ②ほくろ, あざ

□ **moment** 名 ①瞬間, ちょっとの間 ②(特定の)時, 時期 **at that moment** その時に, その瞬間に **at the last moment** 最後の瞬間に, 土壇場で

□ **monkey-faced** 形 猿のような顔をした

□ **monthly** 形 月1回の, 毎月の

□ **mood** 名 気分, 機嫌, 雰囲気, 憂うつ

□ **more** 熟 **more than** 〜以上 **no more** もう〜ない **once more** もう一度

□ **moreover** 副 その上, さらに

□ **Morstan, Captain** モースタン大尉

□ **Morstan, Mary** メアリー・モースタン《人名》

A
B
C
D
E
F
G
H
I
J
K
L
M
N
O
P
Q
R
S
T
U
V
W
X
Y
Z

□ **mostly** 副 主として, 多くは, ほとんど

□ **much** 熟 as much as ～と同じだけ too much 過度の

□ **muddy** 形 泥だらけの, ぬかるみの

□ **murder** 名 人殺し, 殺害, 殺人事件

□ **murderer** 名 殺人犯

□ **muscle** 名 筋肉, 腕力

□ **My God.** おや, まあ

□ **mysterious** 形 神秘的な, 謎めいた

□ **mystery** 名 ①神秘, 不可思議 ②推理小説, ミステリー

N

□ **name no names** (犯罪の共犯者などの) 名前を挙げない

□ **narrowly** 副 ①かろうじて ②狭く, 厳格に

□ **near** 熟 get near 接近する

□ **nearby** 形 近くの, 間近の 副 近くで, 間近で

□ **nearly** 副 ①近くに, 親しく ②ほとんど, あやうく

□ **necessary** 形 必要な, 必然の

□ **need to do** ～する必要がある

□ **needle** 名 針, 針状のもの

□ **neighborhood** 名 近所 (の人々), 付近

□ **neighboring** 形 隣の, 近所の

□ **news** 名 報道, ニュース, 便り, 知らせ

□ **newspaper** 名 新聞 (紙)

□ **next to** ～のとなりに, ～の次に

□ **night** 熟 day and night 昼も夜も sit up all night 徹夜する

□ **no** 熟 no longer もはや～でない [～しない] no matter how どんなに～であろうとも no more もう～ない no one 誰も [一人も] ～ない no one else 他の誰か一人として～しない No problem. いいですよ。どういたしまして。問題ない。 no use 役に立たない, 用をなさない

□ **nobody** 代 誰も [1人も] ～ない

□ **nod** 動 ①うなずく, うなずいて～を示す ②居眠りする

□ **noise** 名 騒音, 騒ぎ, 物音 make noise 音を立てる

□ **none** 代 (～の) 何も [誰も・少しも] …ない

□ **nonsense** 名 ばかげたこと, ナンセンス

□ **nor** 接 ～もまたない

□ **northern** 形 北の, 北向きの, 北からの

□ **Norwood** 名 ノーウッド《地名》

□ **not at all** 少しも～でない

□ **not ～ but ...** ～ではなくて…

□ **not quite** まったく～だというわけではない

□ **not yet** まだ～してない

□ **note** 名 ①メモ, 覚え書き ②注釈 ③注意, 注目 ④手形

□ **nothing** 熟 can do nothing どうしようもない for nothing ただで, 無料で, むだに have nothing to do with ～と何の関係もない know nothing of ～のことを知らない

□ **notice** 名 ①注意 ②通知 ③公告 動 ①気づく, 認める ②通告する

□ **now that** 今や～だから, ～からには

O

□ **oddly** 副 奇妙なことに

□ **of course** 熟 もちろん, 当然

□ **of one's own** 自分自身の

□ **of use** 役に立って

WORD LIST

□ **of which** ～の中で

□ **off** 熟 cut off 切断する, 切り離す drop someone off at home (人)を車で家まで送る far off ずっと遠くに, はるかかなたに go off 出かける, 去る, 出発する off duty 非番[勤務時間外]に[で] off the coast ～沖に[で] off with (すばやく)～を取り去る run off 走り去る, 逃げ去る take off (衣服を)脱ぐ, 取り去る, ～を取り除く, 離陸する, 出発する take the skin off ～から皮膚を引き剥がす walk off 立ち去る

□ **offer** 動 申し出る, 申し込む, 提供する

□ **officer** 名 役人, 公務員, 警察官 police officer 警察官

□ **OK** 名 許可, 承認

□ **on** 熟 and so on ～など, その他もろもろ check on ～を調べる come on ①いいかげんにしろ, もうよせ, さあ来なさい ②(人)に偶然出合う down on one's luck つきに見放されて get on (電車などに)乗る go on 続く, 続ける, 進み続ける, 起こる, 発生する go on to ～に移る, ～に取り掛かる hold on しっかりつかまる keep an eye on ～から目を離さない knock on the door ドアをノックする on behalf of ～のために, ～に代わって on board (乗り物などに)乗って, 搭乗して on each side それぞれの側に on one's way 途中で on one's way to ～に行く途中で on the ground 地面に on the lookout for ～に目を光らせて on the track of ～を追跡[尾行]して on the trail 追跡して on the way 途中で on the way to ～へ行く途中で on top of ～の上(部)に put on ①～を身につける, 着る ②～を…の上に置く sit on ～の上に乗る, ～の上に乗って動けないようにする turn on ①～の方を向く ②(スイッチなどを)ひねってつける, 出す walk on 歩き続ける

□ **once** 熟 at once すぐに, 同時に once more もう一度

□ **one** 熟 at one time ある時には, かつては look from one to the other of us 私たちの顔を代わる代わる見る no one 誰も[一人も]～ない no one else 他の誰一人として～しない one day (過去の)ある日, (未来の)いつか one of ～の1つ[人] this one これ, こちら

□ **oneself** 熟 by oneself 一人で, 自分だけで, 独力で for oneself 独力で, 自分のために put oneself in the position of ～の立場になって考える

□ **onto** 前 ～の上へ[に] lead out onto ～の方へ導く

□ **open** 熟 break open (金庫などを)こじ開ける

□ **open-air** 形 野外の, 戸外の

□ **oppose** 動 反対する, 敵対する

□ **opposite** 形 反対の, 向こう側の 前 ～の向こう側に

□ **or so** ～かそこらで

□ **ordinary** 形 ①普通の, 通常の ②並の, 平凡な

□ **original** 形 ①始めの, 元の, 本来の ②独創的な

□ **other** 熟 each other お互いに look from one to the other of us 私たちの顔を代わる代わる見る

□ **ought** 動《 – to ～》当然～すべきである, きっと～するはずである

□ **out** 熟 be out 外出している carry out 外へ運び出す, [計画を]実行する come out 出てくる, 出掛ける, 姿を現す, 発行される cry out 叫ぶ find out 見つけ出す, 気がつく, 知る, 調べる, 解明する get out ①外に出る, 出て行く, 逃げ出す ②取り出す, 抜き出す go out 外出する, 外へ出る hold out ①差し出す, (腕を)伸ばす ②持ちこたえる, 粘る, 耐える lead out 外へ連れて行く lead out onto ～の方へ導く look out ①外を見る ②気をつける, 注意する look out of (窓などから)外を見る make out 作り上げる, 認識する, 見分ける out

at sea 海で, 海上に **out of** ①〜から外へ, 〜から抜け出して ②〜から作り出して, 〜を材料として ③〜の範囲外に, 〜から離れて ④（ある数）の中から **out of luck** 不運で,（運が）ついていない **out of reach** 手が届かない **pass out**（無料の物を）配る **point out** 指し示す, 指摘する, 目を向ける, 目を向けさせる **pour out** どっと出てくる, 〜に注ぎだす, 吐き出す **pull out** 引き抜く, 引き出す, 取り出す **rush out of** 急いで〜から出てくる **send out** 使いに出す, 派遣する, 発送する **take out** 取り出す, 取り外す, 連れ出す, 持って帰る **think out** 考え抜く, 熟考する

☐ **outburst** 名爆発, 噴出

☐ **outline** 名①外形, 輪郭 ②概略

☐ **over** 熟 **all over** 全て終わって, もうだめで **bend over** 腰をかがめる, 〜に身をかがめる **fall over** 〜につまずく, 〜の上に倒れかかる **go over to** 〜の前に[へ]行く, 〜に出向いて行く **hand over** 手渡す, 引き渡す, 譲渡する **look over at** 〜の方を見る **run over to** 〜へ急いでやってくる, ひと走りする **talk over** 〜について議論する

☐ **overpower** 動圧倒する, 征服する

☐ **overtake** 動①追いつく ②上回る ③車を追い越す

☐ **owe** 動①（〜を）負う,（〜を人の）お陰とする ②（金を）借りている,（人に対して〜の）義務がある

☐ **own** 熟 **of one's own** 自分自身の

☐ **owner** 名持ち主, オーナー

P

☐ **pace** 名歩調, 速度

☐ **package** 名包み, 小包, パッケージ

☐ **paid** 動 pay（払う）の過去, 過去分詞

☐ **painting** 名①絵（をかくこと）, 絵画, 油絵 ②ペンキ塗装

☐ **palm** 名手のひら（状のもの）

☐ **part** 熟 **part with** 〜を手放す **play a part** 役目を果たす

☐ **parted lips** 形半ば開いた唇

☐ **partner** 名配偶者, 仲間, 同僚

☐ **pass out** （無料の物を）配る

☐ **passage** 名①通過, 通行, 通路 ②一節, 経過

☐ **past** 前《時間・場所》〜を過ぎて, 〜を越して 副通り越して, 過ぎて

☐ **path** 名①（踏まれてできた）小道, 歩道 ②進路, 通路

☐ **pay** 動①支払う, 払う, 報いる, 償う ②割に合う, ペイする **pay a visit** 〜を訪問する 名給料, 報い

☐ **peace** 熟 **at peace** 平和に, 安らかに, 心穏やかで

☐ **peaceful** 形平和な, 穏やかな

☐ **pearl** 名真珠

☐ **perfectly** 副完全に, 申し分なく

☐ **performance** 名①実行, 行為 ②成績, できばえ, 業績 ③演劇, 演奏, 見世物

☐ **perhaps** 副たぶん, ことによると

☐ **Pershore** 名パーショア《地名》

☐ **personal** 形①個人の, 私的な ②本人自らの

☐ **pick up** 拾い上げる, 車で迎えに行く, 習得する, 再開する, 回復する

☐ **pile** 名積み重ね,（〜の）山

☐ **pillar** 名①柱, 支柱, 支え ②根幹

☐ **pipe** 名管, 筒, パイプ

☐ **pity** 名哀れみ, 同情, 残念なこと

☐ **plan to do** 〜するつもりである

☐ **plantation** 名大農園, 植林地

☐ **play a part** 役目を果たす

☐ **player** 名①競技者, 選手, 演奏者, 俳優 ②演奏装置

□ **pleasure** 名喜び, 楽しみ, 満足, 娯楽

□ **plenty** 名十分, たくさん, 豊富
plenty of たくさんの〜

□ **point** 熟 **at this point** 現在のところ **point of view** 考え方, 視点 **point out** 指し示す, 指摘する, 目を向ける, 目を向けさせる

□ **poison** 名①毒, 毒薬 ②害になるもの 動毒を盛る, 毒する

□ **poisonous** 形有毒な, 有害な

□ **poker** 名①（トランプで）ポーカー ②火かき棒

□ **police officer** 警察官

□ **police-boat** 名港湾警察が使用する船

□ **policeman** 名警察官

□ **policemen** 名 policeman（警察官）の複数

□ **Pondicherry Lodge** ポンディシェリー荘

□ **pose** 動①ポーズをとる[とらせる] ②気取る, 見せかける ③引き起こす

□ **position** 名①位置, 場所, 姿勢 ②地位, 身分, 職 ③立場, 状況 **put oneself in the position of** 〜の立場になって考える

□ **possibility** 名可能性, 見込み, 将来性

□ **possible** 形①可能な ②ありうる, 起こりうる

□ **possibly** 副①あるいは, たぶん ②《否定文, 疑問文で》どうしても, できる限り, とても, なんとか

□ **postcard** 名（郵便）はがき

□ **pour** 動①注ぐ, 浴びせる ②流れ出る, 流れ込む ③ざあざあ降る **pour out** どっと出てくる, 〜に注ぎだす, 吐き出す

□ **powerful** 形力強い, 実力のある, 影響力のある

□ **powerful-looking** 形屈強そうな

□ **praise** 名賞賛

□ **precious** 形①貴重な, 高価な ②かわいい, 大事な

□ **prepared** 形準備[用意]のできた

□ **previous** 形前の, 先の

□ **price** 名①値段, 代価 ②《-s》物価, 相場

□ **prison** 名①刑務所, 監獄 ②監禁

□ **prisoner** 名囚人, 捕虜

□ **private** 形①私的な, 個人の ②民間の, 私立の ③内密の, 人里離れた

□ **probably** 副たぶん, あるいは

□ **problem** 熟 **No problem.** いいですよ。どういたしまして。問題ない。

□ **proceed** 動進む, 進展する, 続ける

□ **proper** 形①適した, 適切な, 正しい ②固有の

□ **proud** 形①自慢の, 誇った, 自尊心のある ②高慢な, 尊大な

□ **prove** 動①証明する ②（〜であることが）わかる, （〜と）なる

□ **province** 名①州, 省 ②地方, 田舎 ③範囲, 領域

□ **publish** 動①発表[公表]する ②出版[発行]する

□ **pull out** 引き抜く, 引き出す, 取り出す

□ **pull up** 引っ張り上げる

□ **punishment** 名①罰, 処罰 ②罰を受けること

□ **put away** 片づける, 取っておく

□ **put down** 下に置く, 下ろす

□ **put in** 〜の中に入れる

□ **put on** ①〜を身につける, 着る ②〜を…の上に置く

□ **put oneself in the position of** 〜の立場になって考える

□ **puzzle** 動迷わせる, 当惑する[させる]

A B C D E F G H I J K L M N O P Q R S T U V W X Y Z

Q

- □ **quality** 名 ①質, 性質, 品質 ②特性 ③良質
- □ **quantity** 名 ①量 ②《-ties》多量, たくさん
- □ **quarter** 名 ①4分の1, 25セント, 15分, 3カ月 ②方面, 地域 ③部署
- □ **queen** 名 女王, 王妃
- □ **questioning** 形 尋ねるような, 不審そうな
- □ **quickly** 副 敏速に, 急いで
- □ **quietly** 副 ①静かに ②平穏に, 控えめに
- □ **quit** 動 やめる, 辞職する, 中止する
- □ **quite** 熟 not quite まったく～だというわけではない

R

- □ **rabbit** 名 ①ウサギ (兎), ウサギの毛皮 ②弱虫
- □ **ragged** 形 ①ぼろぼろの, ぼろを着た ②ぎざぎざの, ごつごつした
- □ **raise** 動 ①上げる, 高める ②起こす ③～を育てる ④(資金を)調達する
- □ **rajah** 名 ラジャ《[インドの]国王, 支配者》
- □ **rang** 動 ring (鳴る) の過去
- □ **rare** 形 ①まれな, 珍しい, 逸品の ②希薄な ③(肉が)生焼けの, レアな
- □ **rather** 副 ①むしろ, かえって ②かなり, いくぶん, やや ③それどころか逆に rather than ～よりむしろ would rather ～ than … …よりむしろ～したい
- □ **reach** 熟 out of reach 手が届かない within reach of ～の手の届くところに
- □ **ready for** 《be－》準備が整って, ～に期待する

- □ **ready to** 《be－》すぐに [いつでも] ～できる, ～する構えで
- □ **realize** 動 理解する, 実現する
- □ **reason for** ～の理由
- □ **reasoning** 名 推理
- □ **rebellion** 名 反乱, 反抗, 謀反, 暴動
- □ **recognize** 動 認める, 認識 [承認] する
- □ **reconsider** 動 考え直す, 再検討する
- □ **record** 名 ①記録, 登録, 履歴 ②(音楽などの) レコード
- □ **recover** 動 ①取り戻す, ばん回する ②回復する
- □ **rediscovery** 名 再発見
- □ **refreshed** 形 さわやかになって, 再び元気づいて
- □ **relative** 名 親戚, 同族
- □ **release** 動 ①解き放す, 釈放する ②免除する ③発表する, リリースする
- □ **rely** 動 (人が…に) 頼る, 当てにする
- □ **remain** 動 ①残っている, 残る ②(～の) ままである [いる] 名 《-s》①残り (もの) ②遺跡
- □ **remove** 動 ①取り去る, 除去する ②(衣類を) 脱ぐ
- □ **repair** 動 修理 [修繕] する 名 修理, 修繕
- □ **repair yard** 修理場
- □ **repeated** 形 繰り返された, 度重なる
- □ **reply** 動 答える, 返事をする, 応答する
- □ **rescue** 名 救助, 救出
- □ **resistance** 名 抵抗, 反抗, 敵対
- □ **respected** 形 尊敬されている, 評判のいい
- □ **restless** 形 落ち着かない, 不安な

□ **retire** 動引き下がる, 退職 [引退] する

□ **return to** 〜に戻る, 〜に帰る

□ **revenge** 名復讐 **get revenge** 復しゅうする

□ **reward** 動報いる, 報酬を与える

□ **Richmond** 名リッチモンド《地名》

□ **right** 熟 **all right** 大丈夫で, よろしい, 申し分ない, わかった, 承知した

□ **ring** 名①輪, 円形, 指輪 ②競技場, リング **empty ring** 心のこもっていないお祝い

□ **riverside** 名川辺

□ **rob** 動奪う, 金品を盗む, 襲う **rob A of B** AからBを奪う **rob 〜 of ...** 〜から…を奪う

□ **roll** 動①転がる, 転がす ②(波などが)うねる, 横揺れする ③(時が)たつ

□ **romance** 名恋愛(関係・感情), 恋愛 [空想・冒険] 小説

□ **romantic** 形ロマンチックな, 空想的な

□ **roof** 名屋根(のようなもの), 住居

□ **rope** 名綱, なわ, ロープ

□ **rough** 形①(手触りが)粗い ②荒々しい, 未加工の

□ **rub** 動①こする, こすって磨く ②すりむく

□ **ruby** 名ルビー

□ **rudder** 名(船の)かじ

□ **ruined** 形破滅 [壊滅・崩壊] した

□ **run** 熟 **run across** 走って渡る **run along** おいとまする, 立ち去る **run away** 走り去る, 逃げ出す **run in** 走って入る **run into** (思いがけず)〜に出会う, 〜に駆け込む, 〜の中に走って入る **run off** 走り去る, 逃げ去る **run over to** 〜へ急いでやってくる, ひと走りする

□ **rush** 動突進する, せき立てる **rush out of** 急いで〜から出てくる 名突進, 突撃, 殺到

□ **Rutland Island** ラットランド島

S

□ **safely** 副安全に, 間違いなく

□ **sahib** 名閣下, 殿, だんな

□ **said to be** 〜だといわれている, 〜だという話だ

□ **sailor** 名船員, (ヨットの)乗組員

□ **sank** 動 sink (沈む)の過去

□ **sapphire** 名サファイア

□ **scared** 形おびえた, びっくりした

□ **scarf** 名スカーフ

□ **scatter** 動①ばらまく, 分散する ②《be -ed》散在する

□ **scream** 動叫ぶ, 金切り声を出す

□ **sea** 熟 **out at sea** 海で, 海上に

□ **seal** 動印を押す, ふたをする, 密閉する

□ **search** 動捜し求める, 調べる 名捜査, 探索, 調査

□ **searchlight** 名サーチライト, 探照灯

□ **secret** 形①秘密の, 隠れた ②神秘の, 不思議な 名秘密, 神秘

□ **see** 熟 **see for yourself** 自分で確かめる **see if** 〜かどうかを確かめる **see 〜 as ...** 〜を…と考える **you see** あのね, いいですか

□ **seeker** 名追求者

□ **seem** 動(〜に)見える, (〜のように)思われる **seem to be** 〜であるように思われる

□ **selfish** 形わがままな, 自分本位の, 利己主義の

□ **send out** 使いに出す, 派遣する, 発送する

□ **sender** 名送り主, 荷主, 発信人

□ **sense** 名①感覚, 感じ ②《-s》意識,

A B C D E F G H I J K L M N O P Q **R** **S** T U V W X Y Z

正気, 本性 ③常識, 分別, センス ④
意味 **common sense** 常識

□ **sentence** 名①文 ②判決, 宣告

□ **separate** 動①分ける, 分かれる,
隔てる ②別れる, 別れさせる

□ **separately** 副離れて, 独立して,
別々に

□ **sergeant** 名①軍曹, 巡査部長 ②
上級法廷弁護士

□ **serious** 形①まじめな, 真剣な ②
重大な, 深刻な, (病気などが)重い

□ **servant** 名①召使, 使用人, しもべ
②公務員,(公共事業の)従業員

□ **serve** 動①仕える, 奉仕する ②(客
の)応対をする, 給仕する, 食事[飲み
物]を出す ③(役目を)果たす, 務める,
役に立つ

□ **set free** (人)を解放する, 釈放さ
れる, 自由の身になる

□ **set in** (好ましくないことが)始ま
る

□ **set someone thinking** 考え
込ませる

□ **settle** 動①安定する[させる], 落
ち着く, 落ち着かせる ②《– in ～》～
に移り住む, 定住する

□ **shadow** 名①影, 暗がり ②亡霊

□ **shaking** 形震えている, 揺れてい
る

□ **Shall I ～?** (私が)～しましょうか。

□ **shaped** 形(～の)形をした

□ **sharp** 形①鋭い, とがった ②刺す
ような, きつい ③鋭敏な ④急な

□ **sharply** 副鋭く, 激しく, はっきり
と

□ **sheet** 名①シーツ ②(紙などの)1
枚

□ **shelf** 名棚

□ **shelter** 名①避難所, 隠れ家 ②保
護, 避難

□ **Sherlock Holmes** シャーロッ
ク・ホームズ《人名》

□ **shine** 動①光る, 輝く ②光らせる,
磨く

□ **shoeless** 形靴をはかない, 靴なし
の

□ **Sholto, Bartholomew** バー
ソロミュー・ショルトー《人名》

□ **Sholto, John** ジョン・ショルト
ー(少佐)

□ **Sholto, Thaddeus** サディア
ス・ショルトー《人名》

□ **shook** 動shake (振る)の過去

□ **shore** 名岸, 海岸, 陸

□ **shorten** 動短くする, 縮める

□ **short-handed** 形人手不足の

□ **should have done** ～すべきだ
った(のにしなかった)《仮定法》

□ **shoulder** 名肩

□ **show someone in** [人を]中に
案内する, 招き入れる

□ **shown** 動show (見せる)の過去分
詞

□ **shut** 動①閉まる, 閉める, 閉じる
②たたむ ③閉じ込める ④shutの過
去, 過去分詞

□ **side** 名側, 横, そば, 斜面 **on each
side** それぞれの側に

□ **sideburn** 名男性の顔の耳の前に
生えているひげ

□ **Sikh** 名シーク教徒

□ **silence** 名沈黙, 無言, 静寂 **in
silence** 黙って, 沈黙のうちに 動沈
黙させる, 静める

□ **silent** 形①無言の, 黙っている ②
静かな, 音を立てない ③活動しない

□ **sill** 名(窓・戸などの)敷居

□ **similar** 形同じような, 類似した,
相似の

□ **Singapore** 名シンガポール《国
名》

□ **Singh, Mahomet** マホメット・
シン《人名》

□ **sit on** ～の上に乗る, ～の上に乗っ

134

て動けないようにする

□ **sit up all night** 徹夜する

□ **sitting room** 居間, お茶の間

□ **situation** 名 ①場所, 位置 ②状況, 境遇, 立場

□ **skin** 熟 take the skin off ～から皮膚を引き剥がす

□ **sleep in** 熟 寝床に入る, 朝寝坊する, 住み込む

□ **sleep well** よく眠る

□ **sleeve** 名 袖, たもと, スリーブ

□ **slid** 動 slide (滑る) の過去, 過去分詞

□ **slight** 形 ①わずかな ②ほっそりして ③とるに足らない

□ **slip** 動 滑る, 滑らせる, 滑って転ぶ

□ **sloping** 形 傾斜した, 勾配のある

□ **slowly** 副 遅く, ゆっくり

□ **smile at** ～に微笑みかける

□ **Smith** 名 スミス《人名》

□ **smoke** 動 喫煙する, 煙を出す

□ **so** 熟 and so そこで, それだから, それで and so on ～など, その他もろもろ or so ～かそこらで so many 非常に多くの so that ～するために, それで, ～できるように so ～ that ... 非常に～なので…

□ **so-called** 形 いわゆる

□ **sofa** 名 ソファー

□ **soil** 名 土, 土地

□ **soldier** 名 兵士, 兵卒

□ **solid** 形 ①固体 [固形] の ②頑丈な ③信頼できる

□ **solution** 名 ①分解, 溶解 ②解決, 解明, 回答

□ **solve** 動 解く, 解決する

□ **some** 熟 for some time しばらくの間 some time いつか, そのうち

□ **someone** 代 ある人, 誰か

□ **Somerton, Dr.** ソマートン医師《人名》

□ **something** 代 ①ある物, 何か ②いくぶん, 多少

□ **sometimes** 副 時々, 時たま

□ **somewhat** 副 いくらか, やや, 多少

□ **somewhere** 副 ①どこかへ [に] ②いつか, およそ

□ **sorrow** 名 悲しみ, 後悔

□ **sort** 名 種類, 品質 a sort of ～のようなもの, 一種の～

□ **soul** 名 ①魂 ②精神, 心 heart and soul 全身全霊をかけて

□ **southwest** 形 南西の, 南西向きの

□ **spare** 動 ①取っておく ②(～を) 惜しむ, 節約する

□ **speak of** ～を口にする

□ **speak to** ～と話す

□ **sped** 動 speed (急ぐ) の過去, 過去分詞

□ **speed** 名 速力, 速度 動 ①急ぐ, 急がせる ②制限速度以上で走る, スピード違反をする

□ **splash** 動 (水・泥を) はね飛ばす

□ **spotlight** 名 ①スポットライト ②世間の注目

□ **stage** 名 ①舞台 ②段階

□ **stair** 名 ①(階段の) 1段 ②《-s》階段, はしご

□ **stamp** 名 ①印 ②切手

□ **stand by** そばに立つ, 傍観する, 待機する

□ **stand up** 立ち上がる

□ **start** 熟 start doing ～し始める start to do ～し始める with a start ハッとして

□ **state** 名 あり様, 状態

□ **statement** 名 声明, 述べること

□ **steadily** 副 しっかりと

□ **steady** 形 ①しっかりした, 安定した, 落ち着いた ②堅実な, まじめな

□ **steamboat** 名 蒸気船

□ **sticky** 形 ①くっつく, 粘着性の ②暑苦しい ③やっかいな

□ **stiff** 形 ①堅い, 頑固な ②堅苦しい

□ **stolen** 動 steal (盗む) の過去分詞

□ **stone** 名 ①石, 小石 ②宝石

□ **stop by** 途中で立ち寄る, ちょっと訪ねる

□ **storyteller** 名 ①物語をする人, 物語作家 ②うそつき

□ **stranger** 名 ①見知らぬ人, 他人 ②不案内[不慣れ]な人

□ **strengthened** 形 強くする, 丈夫にする

□ **stretch** 動 引き伸ばす, 広がる, 広げる

□ **strike** 動 ①打つ, ぶつかる ②(災害などが) 急に襲う

□ **struck** 動 strike (打つ) の過去, 過去分詞

□ **struggle** 動 もがく, 奮闘する

□ **stubborn** 形 頑固な, 強情な

□ **stuck** 動 stick (刺さる) の過去, 過去分詞

□ **stump** 名 木の切り株, 切れ端

□ **success** 名 成功, 幸運, 上首尾

□ **such a** そのような

□ **such as** たとえば~, ~のような

□ **such ~ as ...** …のような~

□ **such ~ that ...** 非常に~なので…

□ **suggest** 動 ①提案する ②示唆する

□ **suitable** 形 適当な, 似合う, ふさわしい

□ **sum** 名 ①総計 ②金額

□ **sunburned** 形 日焼けした

□ **sunk** 動 sink (沈む) の過去分詞

□ **supper** 名 夕食, 晩さん, 夕飯

□ **supply** 動 供給[配給]する, 補充する 名 供給(品), 給与, 補充

□ **supply-boat** 名 補給船

□ **suppose** 動 ①仮定する, 推測する ②《be -d to ~》~することになっている, ~するものである

□ **sure** 熟 make sure 確かめる, 確認する

□ **surely** 副 確かに, きっと

□ **surprised** 形 驚いた be surprised to do ～して驚く

□ **suspicion** 名 ①容疑, 疑い ②感づくこと

□ **swam** 動 swim (泳ぐ) の過去

□ **swimming** 名 水泳

□ **swing** 動 ①揺り動かす, 揺れる ②回転する, ぐるっと回す

□ **symbol** 名 シンボル, 象徴

□ **sympathy** 名 ①同情, 思いやり, お悔やみ ②共鳴, 同感

T

□ **tail** 名 ①尾, しっぽ ②後部, 末尾

□ **take** 熟 take ~ alive (人・動物などを) 生け捕りにする take all the credit 手柄を独り占めする take back ①取り戻す ②(言葉, 約束を) 取り消す, 撤回する take in 取り入れる, 取り込む, (作物・金などを) 集める take off (衣服を) 脱ぐ, 取り去る, ~を取り除く, 離陸する, 出発する take out 取り出す, 取り外す, 連れ出す, 持って帰る take someone home (人) を家まで送る take the skin off ~から皮膚を引き剥がす take time 時間を取る[かける] take ~ to ... ~を…に連れて行く

□ **tale** 名 ①話, 物語 ②うわさ, 悪口

□ **talk over** ~について議論する

□ **target** 名 標的, 目的物, 対象

□ **task** 名 (やるべき) 仕事, 職務, 課題

□ **taxi** 名 タクシー

- □ **telegram** 名電報
- □ **telegraph** 名電報, 電信
- □ **tell a lie** うそをつく
- □ **tell ~ to ...** ~に…するように言う
- □ **terrified** 形おびえた, こわがった
- □ **Thaddeus Sholto** サディアス・ショルトー《人名》
- □ **than** 前 more than ~以上 rather than ~よりむしろ than usual いつもより would rather ~ than ... …よりむしろ~したい
- □ **thank ~ for** ~に対して礼を言う
- □ **Thank God.** ありがたい
- □ **thankful** 形ありがたく思う
- □ **that** 熟 at that moment その時に, その瞬間に at that time その時 for that matter ついでに言えば now that 今や~だから, ~からには so that ~するために, それで, ~できるように so ~ that ... 非常に~なので… such ~ that ... 非常に~なので…
- □ **theater** 名劇場
- □ **theatre** 名劇場
- □ **them** 熟 both of them 彼ら[それら]両方とも
- □ **then** 熟 by then その時までに just then そのとたんに
- □ **theorist** 名理論家
- □ **theory** 名理論, 学説
- □ **there** 熟 get there そこに到着する, 目的を達成する, 成功する here and there あちこちで
- □ **thieves** 名 thief (泥棒)の複数
- □ **think** 熟 set someone thinking 考え込ませる think of ~のことを考える, ~を思いつく, 考え出す think out 考え抜く, 熟考する
- □ **thinking** 動 think (思う)の現在分詞 名考えること, 思考 形思考力のある, 考える

- □ **this** 熟 at this point 現在のところ by this time この時までに, もうすでに in this way このようにして It's come to this. この始末だ。／ こんなことになってしまった。／ like this このような, こんなふうに this one これ, こちら this way このように
- □ **thorn** 名とげ, とげのある植物, いばら
- □ **those who** ~する人々
- □ **though** 接 ①~にもかかわらず, ~だが ②たとえ~でも as though あたかも~のように, まるで~みたいに even though ~であるけれども, ~にもかかわらず
- □ **thrilling** 形スリル満点の, ぞくぞくする
- □ **throat** 名のど, 気管
- □ **through** 熟 go through 通り抜ける, 一つずつ順番に検討する look through ~をのぞき込む
- □ **throw up** 跳ね上げる
- □ **thrown** 動 throw (投げる)の過去分詞
- □ **tile** 名タイル, 瓦
- □ **time** 熟 all the time ずっと, いつも, その間ずっと at one time ある時には, かつては at that time その時 at times 時には by the time ~する時までに by this time この時までに, もうすでに every time ~するときはいつも for some time しばらくの間 from time to time ときどき some time いつか, そのうち take time 時間を取る[かける] the last time この前～したとき
- □ **tiny** 形ちっぽけな, とても小さい
- □ **tired** 形 ①疲れた, くたびれた ②あきた, うんざりした
- □ **to the last detail** 細かい点の一つ一つに至るまで
- □ **tobacco** 名たばこ
- □ **Toby** 名トビー《犬の名》

137

- □ **Tonga** 名 トンガ《人名》
- □ **tongue** 名 ①舌 ②弁舌 ③言語
- □ **too much** 過度の
- □ **too ~ to …** …するには~すぎる
- □ **top** 熟 on top of ~の上(部)に
- □ **torn** 動 tear(裂く)の過去分詞
- □ **touching** 形 触れ合っている，接触している
- □ **Tower, the** 名 ロンドン塔
- □ **trace** 名 ①跡 ②(事件などの)こん跡 動 たどる，さかのぼって調べる
- □ **tracing** 名 跡を追う[尋ねる]こと
- □ **track** 名 ①通った跡 ②競走路，軌道，トラック on the track of ~を追跡[尾行]して 動 追跡する track down 見つけ出す，追い詰める
- □ **trading ship** 交易船
- □ **tragedy** 名 悲劇，惨劇
- □ **trail** 名 (通った)跡 on the trail 追跡して
- □ **trapdoor** 名 はねぶた，揚げぶた，落とし戸
- □ **treasure** 名 財宝，貴重品，宝物
- □ **treasure-seeker** 名 宝探し家
- □ **treat** 動 ①扱う ②治療する ③おごる
- □ **treatment** 名 ①取り扱い，待遇②治療(法)
- □ **trembling** 形 震える
- □ **trial** 名 ①試み，試験 ②苦難 ③裁判
- □ **trick** 名 ①策略 ②いたずら，冗談③手品，錯覚
- □ **tried** 動 try(試みる)の過去，過去分詞
- □ **trouble** 熟 in trouble 面倒な状況で，困って
- □ **troubled** 形 不安[心配]そうな
- □ **true to** 忠実に
- □ **truly** 副 ①全く，本当に，真に ②心から，誠実に

- □ **trust** 動 信用[信頼]する，委託する
- □ **trusted** 形 信頼されている
- □ **truth** 名 ①真理，事実，本当 ②誠実，忠実さ
- □ **truthful** 形 正直な，真実の
- □ **turban** 名 ターバン
- □ **turn** 熟 turn around 振り向く，向きを変える，方向転換する turn down(音量などを)小さくする，弱くする，拒絶する turn in 向きを変える，(向きを変えてわき道になどに)入る，床につく turn on ①~の方を向く ②(スイッチなどを)ひねってつける，出す turn to ~の方を向く，~に頼る，~に変わる turn white 青ざめる，血の気が引く
- □ **twin** 名 双子の一方，双生児，よく似た1対の人の一方 形 双子の，1対の
- □ **twinkling** 形 きらきら光る
- □ **two** 熟 a ~ or two 1~か2~，2，3の
- □ **tying** 動 tie(結ぶ)の現在分詞

U

- □ **ugly** 形 ①醜い，ぶかっこうな ②いやな，不快な，険悪な
- □ **under arrest** 逮捕されて
- □ **underlie** 動 基礎となる，下に横たわる
- □ **undo** 動 ①ほどく，はずす ②元に戻す，取り消す
- □ **uneasy** 形 不安な，焦って
- □ **unfair** 形 不公平な，不当な
- □ **unfortunately** 副 不幸にも，運悪く
- □ **unique** 形 唯一の，ユニークな，独自の
- □ **unknown** 形 知られていない，不明の
- □ **unless** 接 もし~でなければ，~しなければ

138

WORD LIST

□ **unnatural** 形 不自然な, 異常な

□ **unofficial** 形 非公式な, 私的な

□ **untie** 動 ほどく, 解放する

□ **unusual** 形 普通でない, 珍しい, 見［聞き］慣れない

□ **up** 熟 come up 近づいてくる, 階上に行く, 浮上する, 水面へ上ってくる draw up （車を）止める drive up 車でやって来る follow up （人）の跡を追う get mixed up かかわり合いになる, 巻き添えを食う get up 起き上がる, 立ち上がる go up ①~に上がる, 登る ②~に近づく, 出かける ③（建物などが）建つ, 立つ go up to ~まで行く, 近づく hold up ①維持する, 支える ②~を持ち上げる ③（指を）立てる look up 見上げる, 調べる look up to ~を仰ぎ見る make up one's mind 決心する pick up 拾い上げる, 車で迎えに行く, 習得する, 再開する, 回復する pull up 引っ張り上げる sit up all night 徹夜する stand up 立ち上がる throw up 跳ね上げる up and down 上がったり下がったり, 行ったり来たり, あちこちと up to ~まで, ~に至るまで, ~に匹敵して walk up and down 行ったり来たりする

□ **upon** 前 ①《場所・接触》~（の上）に ②《日・時》~に ③《関係・従事》~に関して, ~について, ~して come upon （人）に偶然出合う look down upon 見下ろす, 俯瞰する look upon ~を見る, 見つめる

□ **uprising** 名 ①起床, 起立 ②反乱, 暴動, 謀反

□ **upset** 形 憤慨して, 動揺して

□ **us** 熟 let us どうか私たちに~させてください look from one to the other of us 私たちの顔を代わる代わる見る

□ **use** 熟 be of use 役に立つ make good use of ~をうまく［有効に］使う no use 役に立たない, 用をなさない of use 役に立って

□ **used** 動 ①use（使う）の過去, 過去分詞 ②《-to》よく~したものだ, 以前は~であった 形 ①慣れている, 《get [become] - to》~に慣れてくる ②使われた, 中古の

□ **usual** 形 通常の, いつもの, 平常の, 普通の as usual いつものように, 相変わらず than usual いつもより

V

□ **valuable** 形 貴重な, 価値のある, 役に立つ

□ **value** 名 価値, 値打ち, 価格 動 評価する, 値をつける, 大切にする

□ **valued** 形 （金銭的に）評価された

□ **variety** 名 ①変化, 多様性, 寄せ集め ②種類

□ **various** 形 変化に富んだ, さまざまの, たくさんの

□ **very well** 結構, よろしい

□ **view** 熟 point of view 考え方, 視点

□ **violently** 副 激しく, 猛烈に, 暴力的に

□ **violin** 名 バイオリン

□ **visit** 熟 pay a visit ~を訪問する

W

□ **waist** 名 ウエスト, 腰のくびれ

□ **waist-belt** 名 腰ベルト

□ **wait for** ~を待つ

□ **walk across** ~を歩いて渡る

□ **walk around** 歩き回る, ぶらぶら歩く

□ **walk off** 立ち去る

□ **walk on** 歩き続ける

□ **walk up and down** 行ったり来たりする

□ **wanted** 形 指名手配される

139

□ **Watson** 名 ワトソン《人名》

□ **wave** 動 ①揺れる, 揺らす, 波立つ ②(手などを振って) 合図する

□ **way** 熟 **by the way** ところで, つ いでに, 途中で **in a firm way** きっ ぱりと **in this way** このようにして **lead the way** 先に立って導く, 案内 する, 率先する **make one's way** 進 む, 行く, 成功する **make way** 道を 譲る[あける], 前進する **on one's way** 途中で **on one's way to** ~ に行く途中で **on the way** 途中で **on the way to** ~へ行く途中で **one's way (to ~)** (~への) 途中で **this way** このように **way to** ~ する方法

□ **wealth** 名 ①富, 財産 ②豊富, 多 量

□ **weigh** 動 ①(重さを) はかる ②重 さが~ある ③圧迫する, 重荷である

□ **well** 熟 **All's well that ends well.** 終わりよければ全てよし。《ことわ ざ》 **as well** なお, その上, 同様に **as well as** ~と同様に **be well -ed** よ く[十分に] ~された **sleep well** よ く眠る **very well** 結構, よろしい

□ **well-known** 形 よく知られた, 有 名な

□ **Westminster Stairs** ウェスト ミンスター・ステアズ《テムズ川に沿 ってある階段の一つ》

□ **wet** 形 ぬれた, 湿った, 雨の

□ **wharf** 名 波止場, 埠頭

□ **what ... for** どんな目的で

□ **whatever** 代 ①《関係代名詞》~ するものは何でも ②どんなこと[も の]が~とも 形 ①どんな~でも ② 《否定文・疑問文で》少しの~も, 何ら かの

□ **where to** どこで~すべきか

□ **which** 熟 **of which** ~の中で

□ **while** 熟 **for a while** しばらくの間, 少しの間

□ **whisky** 名 ウイスキー

□ **whisper** 動 ささやく, 小声で話す

□ **white** 熟 **turn white** 青ざめる, 血 の気が引く

□ **who** 熟 **those who** ~する人々

□ **whoever** 代 ~する人は誰でも, 誰 が~しようとも

□ **whole** 形 全体の, すべての, 完全な, 満~, 丸~

□ **whom** 代 ①誰を[に] ②《関係代 名詞》~するところの人, そしてその 人を

□ **wide** 形 幅の広い, 広範囲の, 幅が ~ある

□ **Wiggins** 名 ウィギンズ《人名》

□ **wild man** 野蛮人

□ **will** 熟 **will have done** ~してしま っているだろう《未来完了形》 **with all the will in the world** 世界中の どんな意志を持ってしても

□ **winding** 形 曲がりくねった

□ **wine** 名 ワイン, ぶどう酒

□ **wish for** 所望する

□ **with** 熟 **be wrong with** (~にとっ て) よくない, ~が故障している **do with** ~を処理する **go with** ~と一 緒に行く, ~と調和する, ~にとても 似合う **have nothing to do with** ~ と何の関係もない **have to do with** ~と関係がある **help ~ with ...** ~ を~の面で手伝う **make friends with** ~と友達になる **off with** (す ばやく) ~を取り去る **part with** ~ を手放す **with a start** ハッとして **with all** ~がありながら **with all the will in the world** 世界中のどん な意志を持ってしても **with fear** 怖 がって

□ **withdraw** 動 引っ込める, 取り下 げる, (預金を) 引き出す

□ **within** 前 ①~の中[内]に, ~の 内部に ②~以内で, ~を越えないで **within reach of** ~の手の届くところ に

□ **woke** 動 wake (目が覚める) の過 去

□ **wonder** 動 ①不思議に思う，(～に) 驚く ②(～かしらと) 思う **wonder if** ～ではないかと思う

□ **wooden** 形 木製の，木でできた

□ **wooden-legged** 形 木の義足の

□ **Worcestershire** 名 ウースターシャー《地名》

□ **worker** 名 仕事をする人，労働者

□ **workman** 名 労働者，職人

□ **workmanship** 名 (職人の) 手腕，優れた技術

□ **workmen** 名 workman (労働者) の複数

□ **world** 熟 **in the world** 世界で **with all the will in the world** 世界中のどんな意志を持ってしても

□ **worn away** 《be－》摩耗する

□ **worried** 形 心配そうな，不安げな **be worried about** (～のことで) 心配している，～が気になる [かかる]

□ **worry about** ～のことを心配する

□ **worse** 形 いっそう悪い，より劣った，よりひどい **get worse** 悪化する

□ **worth** 形 (～の) 価値がある，(～) しがいがある

□ **would like to** ～したいと思う

□ **would rather ～ than ...** …よりむしろ～したい

□ **Would you ～?** ～してくださいませんか。

□ **wrapping** 名 包み

□ **wrinkle** 名 しわ

□ **write down** 書き留める

□ **writing** 名 ①書くこと，作文，著述 ②筆跡 ③書き物，書かれたもの，文書

□ **wrong** 熟 **be wrong with** (～にとって) よくない，～が故障している **go wrong** 失敗する，道を踏みはずす，調子が悪くなる

□ **wronged** 形 不当な扱いを受けた

Y

□ **yard** 熟 **lumber yard** 材木置き場 **repair yard** 修理場

□ **year** 熟 **for years** 何年も **for ～ years** ～年間，～年にわたって

□ **yell** 動 大声をあげる，わめく

□ **yet** 熟 **and yet** それなのに，それにもかかわらず **not yet** まだ～してない

□ **you** 熟 **Could you ～?** ～してくださいますか。 **Would you ～?** ～してくださいませんか。 **you see** あのね，いいですか

□ **yourself** 熟 **see for yourself** 自分で確かめる

English Conversational Ability Test
国際英語会話能力検定

● **E-CATとは…**
英語が話せるようになるための
テストです。インターネット
ベースで、30分であなたの発
話力をチェックします。

www.ecatexam.com

● **iTEP®とは…**
世界各国の企業、政府機関、アメリカの大学
300校以上が、英語能力判定テストとして採用。
オンラインによる90分のテストで文法、リー
ディング、リスニング、ライティング、スピー
キングの5技能をスコア化。iTEP®は、留学、就
職、海外赴任などに必要な、世界に通用する英
語力を総合的に評価する画期的なテストです。

www.itepexamjapan.com

ラダーシリーズ
The Sign of the Four
シャーロック・ホームズ／四つの署名

2024年6月2日　第1刷発行

原著者　コナン・ドイル

発行者　賀川　洋

発行所　**IBCパブリッシング株式会社**
〒162-0804 東京都新宿区中里町29番3号
菱秀神楽坂ビル
Tel. 03-3513-4511　Fax. 03-3513-4512
www.ibcpub.co.jp

印刷　株式会社シナノパブリッシングプレス
装丁　伊藤 理恵　カバーイラスト　田口 智子
落丁本・乱丁本は、小社宛にお送りください。送料小社負担にてお取り替えいたし
ます。本書の無断複写（コピー）は著作権法上での例外を除き禁じられています。

Printed in Japan
ISBN978-4-7946-0817-8